Freud, Jung,
and
Christianity

Freud, Jung, and Christianity

James Forsyth

University of Ottawa Press

Canadian Cataloguing in Publication Data

Forsyth, James, 1930–
Freud, Jung and Christianity

Bibliography: p.
ISBN 0-7766-0212-8

1. Psychology and religion.   2. Theology.
3. Jung, C.G. (Carl Gustave), 1875–1961.
4. Freud, Sigmund, 1856-1939.   5. Christianity.
I. Title.

BL53.F67 1989   200'.1'9   C89-090275-5

UNIVERSITÉ D'OTTAWA   UNIVERSITY OF OTTAWA

This book has been published with the help of a grant from the Canadian
Federation for the Humanities, using funds provided by the Social Sciences and
Humanities Research Council of Canada.

Design: Wendy Kramer

Table of Contents

Preface

This work concerns itself with a particular area of enquiry within the psychology of religion, the dialogue between Christian theology and psychological theory and specifically the depth psychology of Sigmund Freud and Carl Jung. The ongoing dialogue between psychology and theology always seems to stand in need of some kind of methodological clarification. In much of the discussion of "relevance," "parallels," "correlations," "points of intersection," "areas of convergence," "integration," etc., the exact method by which the two disciplines are brought together remains implicit. If the present work has any contribution to make to the methodological debate, it is by way of designating much of the psychology/theology dialogue as an exercise in "natural theology." Hence the first chapter is given over to a discussion of the distinction between the traditional understanding of natural theology (for instance, as rational arguments for the existence of God) and what has been called the "new style" of natural theology. This refers to a natural theology which concerns itself not with questions about God's existence and nature but with locating the dimensions of human existence which give rise to and correlate with the question of God. Its focus, therefore, is not God primarily but human existence, and its aim is not to prove the existence of God but to enquire into the meaningfulness of the concept of God for human existence.

This type of natural theology aims at establishing a correlation between theological concepts such as God, sin, grace, and redemption and the fundamental structures of human existence. To do so is to demonstrate the essential "humanness" of religion. It is the premise of this work that these fundamental structures of human existence are illuminated not only in philosophical thought but also in the work of the great psychological theorists. In this work, therefore, I shall be concerned less with what Freud and Jung have to say about religion than with the fundamental views of human nature and human existence which emerge from their

theories of personality; for the point at which psychological theory
and theological discourse intersect is the field of human experience.
Their common ground consists not so much in what each discipline
has to say about God and religion but in what each says about
human existence. Hence the question of natural theology becomes:
Do the data of psychology and theology refer at any point to the
same type of human experience? It is at the level of human experience that the dialogue takes place, for it is at this level that each
discipline maintains its autonomy. There is then no question of
reducing Christianity to a purely naturalistic religion or of creating
an equally offensive "Christian psychology." If a correlation can
be established, however, between such psychological analyses of
human existence and the data of theological reflection—that is, if
Freudian and Jungian theory reveal dimensions of human existence which correlate with what the theologian is talking about when
he speaks of God, sin, grace, etc.—then one may speak of a psychologically based natural theology.

This type of dialogue, I believe, is a legitimate branch of
the psychology of religion and cannot be simply relegated to the
domain of pastoral psychology. It has the same subject matter (religious experience) as the psychology of religion, with which it is
also methodologically consistent since, in pointing out those correlations between psychological and theological data which make theological concepts humanly meaningful, its method is descriptive
rather than deductive. The present work, however, is not primarily
a book on methodology. I believe that the theories of Freud and
Jung can supply us with interpretive tools by which we may not
only explore the human roots of religion and of the life of faith
but also restore some degree of experiential meaning to some traditional religious and theological concepts. The major portion of this
work, therefore, is given over to a possible Freudian and/or Jungian
"reading" of those concepts.

INTRODUCTION

Natural Theology cannot tell us who and what
God is, but it can trace out the contexts and conditions in human existence and in the world which
correlate to the meaning of the word "God" when
it is used.

Carl E. Braaten, *The Future of God*

Chapter 1
Psychology of Religion as Natural Theology

CONTEMPORARY discussion of the possibility of a natural theology seems to follow one or other of two possible lines of enquiry. The first has to do with the "problem of natural theology." Here we are dealing with natural theology in its traditional meaning as the attempt to demonstrate the existence and nature of God on the basis of human reasoning without the aid of divine revelation, and with the philosophical and theological objections to such an enterprise. A second possible line of enquiry is to bypass this debate about the validity of traditional natural theology and to investigate the possibility of a "new style of natural theology." This would be a type of natural theology which concerns itself not with the existence and nature of God but with locating the area or dimension of human existence and human experience which gives rise to and correlates with the question of God; a natural theology, that is, which does not deal with the question "Does God exist?" but with the question "Why is the human person religious?" In this study, I want to suggest that this latter question is a legitimate one for the psychological study of religion, and to suggest, therefore, the possibility of a psychologically based natural theology.

The natural theology developed by mediaeval theologians such as Anselm and Aquinas was an attempt to discover—to use John B. Cobb, Jr.'s, description—"all that can be known relative to matters of ultimate human concern by reason alone,"[1] as distinct from theology proper, which does not rely solely on human reason but uses reason to systematically interpret the contents of what is first accepted in faith as divine revelation. By methodologically suspending that faith and examining these questions of ultimate concern on the basis of unaided human reason and thereby constructing, for example, rational arguments for the existence of God, the mediaeval theologians hoped to provide a rational support or foundation for religious belief.

It is legitimate to ask why such an enterprise was considered necessary. Why was it necessary to add to the authority of divine revelation the supporting evidence of human reason? To reinforce such a question, all the objections to natural theology could be brought forward: the logical fallacies of its arguments; the impossibility of finding in the material universe evidence for the existence of a reality which transcends that universe; the theological illegitimacy of speaking of the existence of God, on the grounds that God is not an object or being among others whose existence can be debated. These objections certainly seem to have prevailed; but the question of the possibility of a natural theology did not die completely, and this possibility has been pursued by some contemporary scholars such as Charles Hartshorne, John B. Cobb, Jr., and John Macquarrie.[2] Macquarrie, in particular, calls for a "new style" of natural theology, which he describes in general terms as being descriptive rather than deductive and existential rather than rationalistic.[3] This means, as we have already stated, a natural theology which does not "prove" the existence of God (not deductive or rationalistic) but reveals the meaningfulness of the concept of God for human existence (descriptive and existential). In this way, natural theology retains its apologetic function since, as Macquarrie argues, it shows that theological truths "can claim to have foundations in the universal structures of human existence and experience."[4]

This general thrust, however, is shared even by the "old style" of natural theology, for it is precisely this desire to establish a correlation or continuity between the human and the divine, nature and grace, reason and revelation, which accounts, it would seem, for the birth of natural theology. Aquinas, citing St. Paul's statement that "the invisible things of Him are clearly seen, being understood by the things that are made" (Rom. 1:20), argues in a general way that God can be known through his creation as a cause can be known through its effects. Such naturally acquired knowledge of God, he maintains, acts as a preamble to faith, "for faith presupposes natural knowledge, even as grace presupposes nature, and perfection presupposes something that can be perfected."[5] The ultimate justification then for a natural theology and for its apologetic function as a preamble to and support for religious belief is contained in the fundamental Thomist premise that grace does not abolish nature but completes it. By extension, this means that faith completes natural reason and revelation completes the rational arguments for the existence of God. In stating this principle, Aquinas wanted to demonstrate that there was no contradiction between philosophical and theological truth, or, as John Courtney Murray puts it, "to demonstrate that reason is not atheist."[6] Both Aquinas and Macquarrie, both the "old style" and the "new style" of natural theology, have this in common— to reveal the natural foundations of the life of faith in the structures and conditions of human existence.

The attempt to do this by proposing rational arguments for the existence of God became part and parcel of the theistic tradition, so that the Christian community entered the modern era assuming that its religious belief rested on a twofold foundation: divine revelation, which confirmed the conclusions of human reason relative to "matters of ultimate concern." In the modern era, the validity of such a natural theology was severely called into question on philosophical, psychological, and theological grounds.

In their answers to the epistemological question, that is, the question of what is in fact knowable to the human mind, Immanuel Kant (1724–1804) and Auguste Comte (1798–1857) exemplify the philosophical objections to natural theology. For Kant the knowable is that for which there is evidence in the phenomenal world. For Comte the knowable is confined to that which can be discovered through the methods of empirical science. In both cases the knowledge of God is removed from the realm of objective rational knowledge. The psychological attack on natural theology takes the form of an explanation of religious belief as the result of the psychological processes of projection and/or wish-fulfillment. For Ludwig Feuerbach (1804–72) consciousness of God is a stage on the way to human self-consciousness, since God, who is perceived as infinite reason, will, and love, is really a projection or objectification of the essential qualities of human nature raised to an infinite degree. It is through such projection that we become alienated from our own essential nature. God becomes everything, the human person nothing. Only when this projection is withdrawn do we come to the realization that in speaking of God we are really speaking about our own essential nature or, in Feuerbach's famous dictum, theology is really anthropology. For Sigmund Freud (1856–1939) what we project onto the God-image is a deeply rooted psychological need—the need to have, even in adulthood, a loving, protecting father to care for us in the midst of life's harsh realities. For this reason he speaks of God as a surrogate father and of religious belief as an illusion because it is based on wish-fulfillment, not on any kind of objective evidence. For both Feuerbach and Freud the judgement on natural theology's arguments for the existence of God is the same. God is "nothing but" the product of human projection and self-alienation, and belief in God is not supportable by any objective rational arguments. The arguments of natural theology are thereby reduced to rationalizations. Finally, the theological objections to natural theology as stated by Karl Barth (1887–1968) are based on the premise of an infinite qualitative difference between the human and the divine. This means that God cannot be discovered through human reasoning or human experience or human history. The conclusions, therefore, of natural theology are inaccurate and in conflict with the true knowledge of God which can only come through divine revelation. In the face of these attacks on natural theology there are, it would seem, three possible Christian responses.

One is to resist the attack: to continue to insist on the validity of natural theology and the ability of human reason to know God in his existence. Historically, this seems to have been the response of Catholic thinkers, of which *The Problem of God* by John Courtney Murray may be taken as illustrative. Murray takes a negative view of the modern divorce of philosophical from theological truth and finds in it evidence of a modern "will to atheism." Murray distances himself from the position that he attributes to "the contemporary mind particularly within the company of professional philosophers" and "the common Protestant theological disposition," namely, the position that "a natural theology is impossible, that it is impossible for human reason, beginning only with the data of experience, to construct a valid doctrine of God."[7] Against such a view he offers an eloquent defence of the Thomist attempt to synthesize faith and reason and of the possibility of a rational support for religious belief.

A second possible response is to fall back on revelation as the sole foundation of religious belief. This is the position of Karl Barth, who maintained that the hidden God is "wholly other" and is known only through the revelation which takes place in Jesus Christ. There is no natural continuity or analogy of being between God and his creation; the only bridge between God and humanity is the one created by God's intervention in human life and history. There is, therefore, no true knowledge of God apart from divine revelation just as there is no justification and salvation apart from divine grace.

There is a third possible response to the rejection of natural theology. It accepts as valid the objections to traditional natural theology but at the same time is not content to allow religious belief to rest solely on the authority of divine revelation without correlating the objective reality of revelation with a subjective reality which makes it possible for us to receive that revelation. It maintains that if God cannot be known through objective rational arguments, then the human basis for religious belief is something subjective, namely, a subjective experience which makes faith possible.

This third type of response is to be found in the work of theological existentialists such as Sören Kierkegaard, Rudolf Bultmann, and Paul Tillich; but as a tradition within Protestant theology which is preoccupied with establishing the subjective basis of faith it probably begins with Friedrich Schleiermacher (1768–1834). Schleiermacher was intent on making Christian faith self-authenticating, that is, independent of any objective, rational, scientific, or historical argumentation. Religion, he argued, does not originate in the pure impulse to know, for many people, following this impulse, come to accept religious ideas without being particularly religious or "pious." The basis for religious belief was not reason or ideas but the feeling of absolute dependence which characterizes our finite existence and which constituted, for Schleiermacher, an "immediate consciousness of the Deity." The human basis for faith was not to be found in something objective, such as rational argument or empirical evidence, which yield knowledge of the universe, for "religion has nothing to do with this knowledge."[8] Rather, the human basis for faith is subjective, immediate awareness of the infinite—a "sense and taste for the Infinite"[9]—which accompanies our human self-awareness.

This obviously represents a departure from the traditional style of natural theology, which attempted to place religious belief on an objective, rational foundation. Schleiermacher deliberately removed religion from this realm of objective knowledge, and, in speaking to the "cultured despisers" of religion, clearly differentiated between "our faith and your ethics and metaphysics" and between "our piety and what you call morality."[10] It also represents a movement in the direction of a new style of natural theology

since it does not try to demonstrate the objective existence of God
but attempts to identify the dimension or aspect of human existence
(the feeling of absolute dependence) which correlates with the concept of God and makes it meaningful, and therefore makes faith
possible.

It must be pointed out that the shift from a preoccupation
with establishing an objective, rational foundation for faith to a
preoccupation with discovering the subjective, existential, experiential basis of faith goes hand in hand with a more existential
understanding of faith itself. In the Catholic tradition, where that
aspect of faith involving intellectual assent to revealed truth received
considerable emphasis, the traditional style of natural theology with
its objective rational arguments for the existence of God continued
to be regarded as having some validity as a sort of rational preamble
to faith. In this atmosphere a kind of apologetic became popular
in which the preamble to faith was identified as a series of intellectual judgements—"judgements of credibility"—about the validity
of belief in the existence of God and the claims of Christ and the
church. These judgements were seen as creating the possibility of
faith, though they did not account for the believer's act of faith
apart from the role of divine grace.

If, on the other hand, faith is understood more comprehen-
sively as an act, not merely of intellectual assent to revealed truth,
but as the response of the total personality to divine grace, that
is, to the divine act of forgiveness and acceptance, then the act of
faith will be seen as also involving affective trust and existential
commitment. By the same token, the preamble to faith, that is,
the human experience which creates the possibility of faith, will
be seen not merely as a series of intellectual judgements by which
we are disposed to believe certain truths, but as a series of existential
or psychological states by which we are disposed to accept and trust
in a message of forgiveness, love, and acceptance. In the work of
theological existentialists such as Kierkegaard, Bultmann, and
Tillich we can observe this preoccupation with identifying the subjective experience or series of experiences which constitute the
preamble to faith.

The question that Schleiermacher had tried to answer was:
How do we come to a knowledge of the transcendent reality of God
apart from revelation and apart also from the rational demonstrations of traditional natural theology? What aspect of our human

existence creates the awareness of God? Schleiermacher's answer was: the human experience of absolute dependence. Existentialist thinkers such as Sören Kierkegaard and Rudolf Bultmann answered the same question with reference to the experience of awareness of and responsibility for one's existence. In their view faith is not the conclusion of a rational argument but an existential decision and commitment which become possible at critical points in one's concrete existence as, for example, when one becomes acutely aware of the inadequacy of all human attempts at moral rectitude (Kierkegaard) or the failure of human idealism or the human striving for self-actualization (Bultmann). But it is perhaps in the answer which Paul Tillich (1886–1965) gives to this question that we perceive most clearly the beginnings of a new style of natural theology.

Tillich's analysis of the Christian faith experience takes place within the context of his description of the three possible ways in which the individual may relate to himself and to the world, which he describes as three types of courage: the courage to be as part; the courage to be as oneself; and the courage of confidence, which is the courage of faith. These three types of courage may likewise be seen as three existential states experienced by the believer in the movement towards faith existence, that is, the level of human existence achieved by one whose life is rooted in the experience of grace and faith.

The courage to be as part is the courage one achieves in a heteronomous situation. It is the courage and security which result from identifying with and submitting to a strong authority figure, but it is a security purchased at the price of one's identity and individuality. In a heteronomous relationship one finds the "courage to be," that is, the courage to affirm one's own existence, only by making that existence part of something or someone greater than oneself through abject submission, submerging one's individuality in the collectivity, or through social conformity. The courage to be as oneself is, by contrast, the courage of autonomy, the affirmation of the self as a self, but achieved at the price of genuine participation in one's world. This type of self-affirmation together with the affirmation of one's self as part reveal, for Tillich, our existential condition, for both are aspects of human self-affirmation.

This twofold self-affirmation—as individual and as participant—reflects an existential split in our being. As a self, one is part of one's world but at the same time separated from it. Just as one's existence is torn between individuality and participation, so one's self-affirmation oscillates between the courage to be as oneself and the courage to be as part. This existential split and the resulting anxiety demand a form of courage which transcends both the courage of individualization and the courage of participation. In other words, since one cannot find the basis of self-affirmation in oneself or in one's world, both must be transcended. What must be discovered is that courage which is "rooted in a power of being that is greater than the power of oneself and the power of one's world."[11] This is the power of being which overcomes the insecurity and threat of non-being or nothingness inherent in finite being.

For Tillich, this third type of courage is the courage of faith, which is the courage to "accept acceptance." Faith is confidence in the divine acceptance and forgiveness; therefore, the courage which results from faith is derived neither from oneself nor from one's world. Faith involves the renunciation of all such finite sources of security. The source of this forgiveness and acceptance is the ground and power of being itself, and therefore it permits one to affirm one's own being in a way which transcends individuality and participation, oneself and one's world:

> Faith is not an opinion but a state. It is the state of being grasped by the power of being which transcends everything that is and in which everything that is participates. He who is grasped by this power is able to affirm himself because he knows that he is affirmed by the power of being itself.[12]

Thus, for Tillich, faith is a "theonomous" experience, since the courage to affirm one's own existence is derived neither from an alien source (one's world) nor from a shallow source (one's self) but from a source which transcends both, but transcends them as their ultimate depth and meaning.

Whence then comes the awareness of God? For Tillich, the human basis for faith is, again, not our rational capacity, or rational reflection on our world, or rational arguments from the world to God, but the human capacity for what he calls "ultimate concern," that is, the concern for what is ultimate, infinite, or absolute. In

the context of his analysis of faith as courage, this means our desire
for a source of courage which transcends the finite sources of self
and world and, therefore, overcomes the existential split in our self-
affirmation between self as participant and self as autonomous individual. Only an ultimate, transcendent reality can be the source
of the "courage of confidence."

But how do we come to a knowledge of such a transcendent
reality apart from the rational demonstrations of natural theology?
Tillich's answer to this question suggests a new style of natural theology for it represents, to use Tillich's distinction, a shift from the
"cosmological method" to the "ontological method," which in
Tillich's words "is neither an argument, nor does it deal with the
existence of God."[13] In the ontological method, God is encountered not through a process of objective reasoning (the cosmological
method), but as a matter of immediate awareness. This God is not,
Tillich says, the *ens realissimum* (the highest among all beings) but
the *primum esse* (the ground of being in which all particular beings
participate). God is not an object discovered by a knowing subject;
he is that which transcends and precedes the distinction between
subject and object, the principle of being in which both subject and
object participate. Our awareness of God, he argues, is in the first
instance the awareness of something unconditioned or absolute
which accompanies our own self-awareness. This awareness or
"ultimate concern" can be described but not proved by any rational
argument. Rational arguments only prove the existence of some
objective reality, whereas the awareness of God as a component
of our own self-consciousness must be "independent of any
encounter with our world."[14]

In the light of Tillich's distinction, the post-Kantian rejection
of traditional theism on the grounds that the physical universe gives
no evidence for the existence of God would seem to be a rejection
of the cosmological method by which believers tried to give rational
support to their religious belief through objective, rational demonstrations of God's existence. Accordingly, the Christian response,
which we have been discussing, to this undermining of traditional
natural theology has been, to a large extent, a reaffirmation of the
ontological method—an attempt to make faith self-authenticating
and independent of objective rational arguments. It was necessary,
therefore, to describe the subjective foundation of religious belief
which made faith "independent of any encounter with our world."

This movement, which as we have seen began with Schleiermacher, attempted to place our experience of God beyond the subject-object split that was the basis of traditional natural theology. If the awareness of God is an accompaniment of our own self-awareness, it becomes self-authenticating, that is, independent of any scientific, historical, or rational demonstration. The foundation on which faith is built is now something subjective, such as the "feeling of absolute dependence" (Schleiermacher) or the experience of "ultimate concern" (Tillich). The attempt to describe this subjective basis for faith points to a new style of natural theology.

It would seem that what Tillich has done is to remove God from the realm of objective reality knowable through rational, scientific, or historical demonstration; and he has done so on theological grounds, namely, through an understanding of God as a reality transcending the subject-object dichotomy and therefore not knowable as an object whose existence can be proved. What remains within the capability of human reason is, in Tillich's words, "the rational description of the relation of our mind to Being as such."[15] In other words, God, understood as being itself, cannot be proved to exist as *a* being. All we can do is describe that aspect of human nature or human existence (e.g., Tillich's "ultimate concern") which correlates with this new understanding of God, and this is to give a new meaning to natural theology.

Natural theology in any sense deals with the human side of the divine-human encounter, that is, with what makes the human person receptive to divine revelation. The old style of natural theology identified this as the capacity of human reason to demonstrate God's existence. Thus revelation was seen to coincide with and be an extension of the conclusions of human reasoning. The contemporary theological view seems to be that natural theology, in this traditional sense, retains a certain validity to the extent that it is seen as having a propaedeutic function in regard to theology proper; that is, when it is seen not as setting up a source of knowledge independent of revelation but as identifying the human capacity that correlates with divine revelation. In accounting for the endurance of the natural theology of Aquinas, T. F. Torrance points out that Aquinas' natural theology was "firmly correlated with the body of theology proper. . . . St. Thomas' achievement was to establish the fact that if knowledge of God is to be actualized in us it requires a rational counterpart to it in our structured under-

standing of it, firm enough to merit philosophical analysis and consideration on its own."[16] E. L. Mascall moves the Thomistic
natural theology even closer in its meaning to the new style of
natural theology by arguing that the five ways of Aquinas are not
to be seen as formal arguments for the existence of God but as
demonstrations of the radical inability of finite being to account
for its own existence. "The Five Ways," he maintains, "are therefore not so much five different demonstrations of the existence of
God as five different methods of manifesting the radical dependence of finite being upon God, of declaring, in Dom Pontifex's
phrase, that the very essence of finite being is to be effect-implying
cause."[17]

    To interpret the old style of natural theology in this way is,
to put it simply, to interpret it as saying something about human
existence rather than about God as such. Such an interpretation
serves two purposes in the context of our present discussion. First,
it moves in the direction of answering the theological objections
of Barth and others regarding natural theology. Andrew Louth,
for example, argues that what Barth really objected to was not so
much natural theology as natural religion.[18] If natural theology is
understood as based on a presupposition by theologians that "by
the light of natural reason they could know enough about God to
be able to worship him adequately and save their souls,"[19] then
it becomes the basis for a natural religion, and this is what Barth
rejects as leading to idolatry. But if natural theology simply points
to the rational capacity to know God, then it refers only to the subjective foundation of faith, and one can accommodate Barth's objections by pointing out that this capacity to know God, left to itself,
falls into error and idolatry unless it is completed by divine
revelation.

    Secondly, this interpretation of traditional natural theology
brings it closer in meaning to what we have been calling the "new
style" of natural theology. If Aquinas is not trying to prove the
existence of God but to point out that the radically dependent nature
of finite being logically implies a cause or creator, then he does
not differ substantially from Tillich, who maintains that the finite
world "points beyond itself." For Tillich, God is not transcendent
in the sense of being "above" the finite; he is transcendent in the
sense that he is the transcendent depth and ground of all finite being
and of all human experience. Consequently we do not discover God

by looking away from the world and our own human existence; on the contrary, we discover God precisely as the ultimate depth dimension of our human experience:

> To call God transcendent in this sense does not mean that one must establish a "superworld" of divine objects. It does mean that, within itself, the finite world points beyond itself. In other words, it is self-transcendent.[20]

That to which reality or being points is its ultimate depth or ground. God is discovered not by looking up and away from reality but by looking into the depth of reality and of human experience. When we do this, Tillich argues, we encounter our own finitude; and only by discovering the boundary or limit of our own finitude, that is, of human possibility, can we discover what is unconditional or infinite.

This point at which we discover the infinite in the depths of our finite being, at which the infinite touches the finite, is what Tillich calls the "boundary situation." It is the point where, realizing the finite, limited nature of all human activity and fulfillment, we are threatened by non-being and genuine faith becomes possible. For to have faith means "to be grasped by the power of being itself";[21] it means to be able to affirm one's existence because at the depths of that existence one has encountered the ground and power of being itself, in which all particular beings participate and which constitutes the "Yes" that sustains us in the face of the "No" we experience as the result of the limitations of our finite being. But the affirmation can be experienced only by experiencing the negation; the reality, only by experiencing the nothingness; the unconditioned, only by experiencing the conditioned; the Yes, only by experiencing the No:

> Religion is an experience of the Unconditioned and that means an experience of absolute reality on the ground of the experience of absolute nothingness; it will experience the nothingness of all existing things, the nothingness of values, the nothingness of personal life; where this experience has led to the absolute, radical No, there it shifts into an equally absolute experience of reality, into a radical Yes.[22]

All this does not obscure the difference between the thought of Aquinas and that of Tillich. Aquinas' God is the supreme being; Tillich's God is being itself. Aquinas' approach is objective, rational, cosmological; Tillich's approach is subjective, experiential, onto-logical. Aquinas believes that the dependent, limited quality of finite being creates the possibility of a rational argument for the existence of a transcendent reality; Tillich believes that the experience of limitation and finitude of itself leads to an experience of that transcendent reality. What they seem to have in common, however, is the conviction that the starting point for the human knowledge of God is the self-transcending quality of finite being, that quality by which it "points beyond itself." Perhaps, therefore, the most general statement we could make about natural theology is that it attempts to identify and analyze the quality of self-transcendence which characterizes finite being in general and human existence in particular and which correlates with the concept of a transcendent reality or God. It is this quality of self-transcendence—as the natural and human basis for belief in a transcendent God—and not God as such which is the primary object of natural theology.

If this description is valid for all types of natural theology, what then differentiates the "new style" of natural theology from natural theology in its more traditional form? As we have seen, the old style of natural theology identified the human basis for religious belief as the rational capacity to know God. The new style of natural theology does not isolate the rational faculty of the human person but correlates the conditions of human existence as such with the concept of God. Such a natural theology takes what is implied, for example, in the natural theology of Aquinas—the self-transcending quality of finite being—and makes it the explicit object of its study. It stops short, therefore, of attempting to prove the existence of God and deals rather with the question "Why is the human person religious?" Moreover, in trying to answer this question, it does not look for the human basis of religion only in the rational faculty but, again as we have seen, in the conditions and structures of human existence in general. Thus, while Aquinas tried to demonstrate the essential *rationality* of religion, Tillich deals with the essential *humanness* of religion.

This type of natural theology does not prove the existence of God, for only faith can affirm that in pointing beyond itself human existence does in fact point to a transcendent God as the object of its striving for self-transcendence; but it does try to demonstrate that the goal of one's religious striving is consistent with one's deepest human aspirations—that the religious goal is not antithetical to the human, nor something merely "tacked on" to our human growth, but represents the transcendent goal of human becoming. In analyzing the self-transcending quality of human existence, natural theology attempts to identify the "religious dimension" of human existence, namely, that dimension which correlates with theology's understanding of God. John Macquarrie describes the function of such a natural theology as providing a "link between secular thought and theology proper," since it is in the data of "secular thought" that we find an analysis of human nature and existence which draws attention "to those structures and experiences which lie at the root of religion and of the life of faith."[23]

In attempting to formulate such a natural theology, Macquarrie turns to the existentialist philosophy of Martin Heidegger for an analysis of human existence. Charles Hartshorne and John B. Cobb, Jr., on the other hand, want to construct a natural theology on the basis of Alfred North Whitehead's process philosophy.[24] What is being sought in all these attempts at formulating a natural theology is a philosophical view of reality in general or of human existence in particular which correlates and is consistent with a Christian theological point of view. It is just such an analysis of human existence which forms the basis of contemporary theologies such as the theology of hope and the theology of liberation. For the theology of hope, the self-transcending quality of human existence is its hope for the future. In its hope for a better future, human existence "points beyond itself" to a future state which transcends the limitations of the present. For the theology of liberation, the self-transcending quality of human existence is found in the human struggle for liberation from social, economic, and political oppression—from everything, in short, which limits human freedom and fulfillment. Both theologies begin with an analysis of human existence which correlates with and makes meaningful the biblical God of the future, of the Exodus, and of Christian eschatology. I want to suggest, however, that this analysis of the self-transcending quality of human existence, which forms the basis of natural theology, is not the exclusive domain of philosophy but is also the task of the social sciences. Thus the social sciences in general and, in the context of our discussion, psychology in particular can be seen as a basis for a natural theology, as natural theology is presently understood.

Implicit in any psychological theory there is a psychological anthropology—a fundamental view of human nature or the human condition. Many psychological theorists have also proposed theories of religion. Natural theology is less interested in these theories of religion than in theories of personality as such, for it is there that we shall find that analysis of human existence which perhaps correlates with theological truth, and of the experience of self-transcendence which in another context might be described as a religious experience. It is precisely at this level of human existence and human experience that psychological and theological discourse intersect in the sense that they represent different ways of interpreting or conceptualizing the same human experience. This type of experience which can be interpreted both psychologically and theologically is what Erich Fromm has called the "x-experience."[25] The dialogue between psychology and religion, therefore, has as its aim a fuller understanding of the human experience which both disciplines attempt to interpret and conceptualize. Hence the possibility is created of a mutually enriching dialogue in which the psychologist recognizes the symbolic value of the religious language of rebirth and salvation, and the theologian recognizes the value of the psychological analysis of the dynamics of human personality for a fuller understanding of the human experience reflected in such terms as "God," "justification," "salvation," "redemption," "grace." In the words of Seward Hiltner: "If the study of theology consists of God, man, sin and salvation—then the kind of psychological understanding which is now becoming possible is related to all four fields. In other words, there is a sense in which psychological knowledge is an aspect of all theological knowledge."[26]

To take an obvious example, for the Christian believer the core of his faith and the paradigm for the interpretation of his own life experience is the death and resurrection of Christ. This is the central symbol, which conveys a fundamental truth—that, in some sense, we must die in order to live. The new style of natural theology would see in the Freudian analysis of the conflict between the life instinct (Eros) and the death instinct a description of the human condition which renders this central Christian symbol of death and rebirth meaningful for human existence; for that symbol addresses itself to the ultimate religious question, which Freud saw as the ultimate human question: Can life triumph over death? Whereas for Freud the goal of the life instinct was interpersonal unity or

community and ultimately the "unity of all mankind," for Carl
Jung the pursuit of life is described as a quest for intrapsychic wholeness. This involves an assimilation of unconscious contents of the
psyche into our conscious life and attitudes. The centre of personality thus shifts from the ego (the centre of consciousness) to the
"self" (the centre of the total personality embracing both consciousness and the unconscious). This shift involves what Jung does not
hesitate to call a "crucifixion of the ego." Both of these psychological
models of human becoming render the central Christian symbol
of death and resurrection meaningful for human existence, and
restore some degree of experiential meaning to the truth it conveys.

A dialogue, therefore, between psychology and theology has
at least two important results. First, it creates the possibility of a
psychologically based natural theology insofar as we can discover
in psychological theory an analysis of the self-transcending quality
of human existence which correlates with theology's understanding
of God. Secondly, it creates the possibility of restoring an experiential meaning to traditional religious concepts such as sin, grace,
and redemption which may have become so objectified as to lose
their connection with the human experience conveyed by such
terms. To explore these dimensions of human existence is not only
to explore the human roots of religion and the life of faith, but also
to restore some degree of experiential meaning to those theological
concepts. This, it seems to me, is consistent with the aims of what
we have been calling the new style of natural theology—in this
instance, a psychologically based natural theology.

In order to do this it is necessary to look beyond a narrow
conception of psychology as a medical discipline whose aim is the
alleviation of mental illness through rational analysis and to explore
psychological theory at that point where it deals with the fundamental nature and meaning of human existence. If it be argued
that this takes us beyond psychology proper, we can only respond
by pointing out that the great psychological theorists seemed to have
gone beyond the limits of such a narrowly conceived psychology
and dealt with more fundamental questions of meaning. Ira Progoff
has argued that such a widening of psychology's "spiritual horizons" happened of necessity if psychology was to answer the fundamental problems which brought it into existence.[27]

It is at this level, where psychological theory touches upon
the spiritual nature of human personality and the fundamental

meaning of human existence, namely, at that point where psychology "points beyond itself," that it is able "to fulfill the purpose inherent in its historical existence," which is to help modern man to discover the meaning of his life "by guiding him to an experience that is beyond psychology."[28] It is at this point also that psychological theory can serve as the basis for a natural theology, for there psychology discovers, again in Progoff's words, that "man's psychological nature suggests something transcendent of which the psyche is but a partial reflection."[29]

In the chapters that follow an attempt will be made to work out such a psychologically based natural theology by exploring the "universal structures of human existence and experience" that are implied in the psychological theories of Sigmund Freud and Carl Jung. In doing so, our purpose will be twofold: (1) To reveal to what extent each theory in its own right provides a view of human existence which correlates with theological truth (i.e., to what extent each theory contains an implicit natural theology). (2) To suggest that these two theories complement each other as interpretive tools for the understanding of Christian existence.

NOTES

1. John B. Cobb, Jr., *A Christian Natural Theology* (London: Lutterworth Press, 1965), p. 259.
2. See Charles Hartshorne, *A Natural Theology for Our Time* (Lasalle, Ill.: Open Court, 1967); Cobb, *A Christian Natural Theology*, and John Macquarrie, *Principles of Christian Theology* (New York: Scribner's, 1966).
3. Macquarrie, *Principles of Christian Theology*, pp. 48–52.
4. Ibid., p. 35.
5. *Summa Theologiae*, Pt. 1, Qu. 2, A. 2.
6. John Courtney Murray, *The Problem of God* (New Haven: Yale University Press, 1964), p. 75.
7. Ibid., p. 74.
8. Friedrich Schleiermacher, *On Religion: Speeches to Its Cultured Despisers*, trans. John Oman (New York: Harper Torchbooks, 1958), p. 35.
9. Ibid., p. 39.
10. Ibid., p. 34.
11. Paul Tillich, *The Courage to Be* (London: Fontana, 1962), p. 152.
12. Ibid., p. 168.

13.Paul Tillich, *Theology of Culture* (New York: Oxford University Press, 1964), p. 15.
14.Paul Tillich, *A History of Christian Thought* (London: SCM Press, 1968), p. 165.
15.Tillich, *Theology of Culture*, p. 15.
16.T. F. Torrance, "The Problem of Natural Theology in the Thought of Karl Barth," *Religious Studies* 6 (1970): 132–33.
17.E. L. Mascall, *Existence and Analogy* (London: Longmans Green and Co., 1949), p. 71. Whether or not one agrees with Mascall's interpretation of the "five ways" of Aquinas, the important point, in the context of this discussion, is that such an interpretation is obviously inspired by a new understanding of natural theology.
18.Andrew Louth, "Barth and the Problem of Natural Theology," *Downside Review* 87 (1969): 268–77.
19.Ibid., p. 270.
20.Paul Tillich, *Systematic Theology*, 3 vols. (Chicago: University of Chicago Press, 1951–1963), 2:7.
21.Tillich, *The Courage to Be*, p. 153.
22.Paul Tillich, as quoted in James Luther Adams, *Paul Tillich's Philosophy of Culture, Science and Religion* (New York: Harper and Row, 1965), p. 43.
23.Macquarrie, *Principles of Christian Theology*, p. 35.
24.See Hartshorne, *A Natural Theology for Our Time*; and Cobb, *A Christian Natural Theology*.
25.Erich Fromm, *You Shall Be As Gods* (New York: Holt, Rinehart and Winston, 1966), pp. 56–60.
26.Seward Hiltner, "The Psychological Understanding of Religion," *Crozer Quarterly* 24 (1947): 36.
27.Ira Progoff, *The Death and Rebirth of Psychology* (New York: McGraw-Hill, 1956), pp. 14–15.
28.Ibid., p. 259.
29.Ibid., p. 256.

FREUD AND CHRISTIANITY

This struggle is what all life essentially consists of,
and the evolution of civilization may therefore be
simply described as the struggle for life of the
human species.

Sigmund Freud, *Civilization and Its
Discontents*

For to me to live is Christ, and to die is gain.

St. Paul, Philippians 1:21

Chapter 2
Faith and the Human Condition

THE two discoveries of Freud which are most basic to his theory of personality and which, in his own lifetime, were most controversial are: the concept of the unconscious (that is, the contention that mental processes are essentially unconscious, and that conscious processes are isolated parts of the whole psychic entity); and the theory that human instinctual life—with particular emphasis on the sex instinct—plays a basic and predominant role not only in the causation of nervous and mental disorders, but also in human cultural and social achievements. Freud himself viewed the discoveries of psychoanalysis as the most recent of three great attacks by science on humanity's "naive self-love."[1] The first was the discovery by Copernicus that our earth was not the centre of the universe; the second was the biological theory of evolution associated with Charles Darwin, which deprived the human species of the privilege of having been specially created; and the third is the psychoanalytic theory of personality, which informs us that we are not even masters of our own inner life, that we are subject to motives and impulses of which we are unconscious.

Since Christianity, in order to make its message relevant and intelligible to the human community, must take into account the discoveries of the natural and social sciences according to which humanity understands itself, a dialogue between Christianity and psychoanalysis was inevitable. In that dialogue at least three possible readings of Freudian theory can be discerned. As a psychology of religion which interprets religion as a regressive illusion and an obsessional neurosis, Freudian theory has predictably drawn a defensive and apologetic response from Christian scholars. Some apologists have emphasized Freud's personal animosity towards religion or his incomplete knowledge of religion. But it is not sufficient to simply dismiss Freud's critique of religion on the grounds that he was, according to Ernest Jones's description, an "unrepentant atheist," or on the grounds of his alleged limitations as a student of religion. Freud himself confessed that when he spoke of religion he was concerned with what the ordinary person understands by his religion.

What Freud discovered in the ordinary person's understanding and practice of religion was frequently explainable only in the context of his theory of neurosis, and this has provided a second avenue of dialogue for the Christian scholar. As a theory of neurosis Freudian theory has provided a basis for the work of the pastoral psychologist in identifying neurotic distortions of the Christian life, and thereby distinguishing between authentic and inauthentic expressions of Christian faith. Real dialogue, however, can result only from a common preoccupation or focus of concern. In the case of Christian theology and Freudian theory that common concern, I believe, runs deeper than the attempt to account for neurotic distortions of the Christian life; for at a third and more profound level, namely, the level of psychological anthropology in dialogue with theological anthropology, both Freudian and Christian thought are concerned with the fundamental question: Can life prevail over death? It is at this level that a convergence of Freudian theory and Christian theology is discernible, for in locating the source of human discontent not in the subject-object duality of the individual and society but in the duality to be found in human nature itself—the "eternal struggle of Eros and the death instinct"—Freud gives that discontent a tragic kind of inevitability which, in this respect at least, is in accord with the Christian doctrine of sin.

It is necessary, therefore, to go beyond Freud's theory of religion and his theory of neurosis and confront the essentials of psychoanalytic theory, for what Freud says about the fundamental human condition is more important for dialogue with Christianity than what he says about God and religion. What we shall concentrate on, therefore, in the following pages is his theory of instincts and his theory of civilization for it is here that Freud deals with the ultimate religious question: the question of the possibility of life in the face of the tragic inevitability of death. It is precisely Freud's analysis of the tragic dimension of human existence which correlates with the Christian concepts of sin and grace, fall and redemption. What he says about the conflict of life and death within human existence cannot be ignored by a religious tradition whose central theme is one of death and resurrection and whose ultimate promise is one of the triumph of life over death.

It is this tragic dimension of life which must be experienced
if a message of salvation is to have any meaning. In a meditation
on Psalm 90, Paul Tillich describes the human condition as a conflict
of tragedy and hope.[2] The transitoriness of life gives it a tragic
dimension; but the religious person is described as the one in whom
"hope supersedes tragedy." Tragedy, moreover, is a precondition
of hope: only the person who is aware of the tragic nature of existence seeks fulfillment in something transcending that existence.
Only those who are discontented with the present reality hope for
a new reality, not simply because of the discontent, but because
their discontent brings them to that "boundary situation" in which
consciousness of finitude leads to awareness of the infinite.

The reality of the infinite ground of one's being is experienced only in the depths of one's finite being; realizing the finite,
limited nature of all human activity and fulfillment, we are threatened by non-being. For Tillich, as we have seen, religion is the
experience of being "grasped by the power of being itself,"[3] and
its precondition is the full awareness of the limitations of one's finite
existence. Religion is "an experience of absolute reality on the
ground of the experience of absolute nothingness."[4]

A similar insistence on the awareness of finitude as a precondition for an awareness of the infinite appears in the writings
of Jung, who maintains that it is only by becoming aware of the
narrow limits of individual consciousness that we can forge a link
to the limitlessness of the unconscious. "In knowing ourselves,"
he argues, "to be unique in our personal combination—that is,
ultimately limited—we possess also the capacity for becoming conscious of the infinite. But only then!"[5] Whether we call this tragic
dimension of life a sense of finitude, of limitation, of nothingness,
or of the transitoriness of life, it is precisely the awareness of this
"negative tragic principle" which, according to William James,
gives the religious consciousness of the "twice-born" or "sick soul"
a certain richness and completeness which are lacking in the more
"healthy minded" religious personality.[6] This sensitivity to evil,
says James, may exist at two levels. There are those for whom evil
consists of a "maladjustment with things" (subject-object duality),
while for others evil is a "wrongness or vice in [their] essential
nature."[7]

We may conclude that an analysis of the tragic dimension
of life is a precondition of any religious message of hope. It is for

this reason that I have been suggesting that Freud's greatest contribution to the psychology of religion was not so much his studies
of the origins of religious belief in *The Future of an Illusion* and *Totem
and Taboo*, but rather his analysis of the tragic dimension of human
existence—of human discontent—in *Beyond the Pleasure Principle* and
Civilization and Its Discontents. What makes this analysis particularly
significant for dialogue with Christian theology is Freud's insistence
that the source of human discontent—of the tragic nature of life—is
not the conflict between the individual and society (James's "maladjustment with things") but the conflict or duality to be found within
human nature itself; and that this conflict could ultimately be
described in categories which Freudian theory shares with Christian
thought—the categories of life and death, Eros and the death
instinct. It is in Freud's treatment of human instinctuality and in
his theory of civilization or culture that we find most explicitly this
analysis of the tragic dimension of human existence.

The Theory of Instincts

The Freudian analysis of the human condition may be summarized
in three words: dualism, repression, and discontent. The discontent
of civilized humanity results from the instinctual renunciation—
repression and sublimation—which civilization demands of us. But
the ultimate source of this repression—and what gives it its inevitable and tragic character—is not civilization itself but the duality
inherent in human nature. Humanity's problem is not ultimately
the repressive force of cultural and social institutions but the repression which results from the instinctual conflict or duality within
individual human nature.

Throughout the development and various formulations of
Freud's instinct theory he remained committed to a model of human
nature which was dualistic and conflictual; human nature and
behaviour were to be explained in terms of the conflict of opposing
instincts. In attempting to describe the poles of that duality his
theory seems to have evolved through three distinct phases or formulations. In the first formulation of the theory Freud identified two
conflicting groups of instincts: the sex instinct, which represents
the psychic energy which Freud termed "libido," and the ego
instincts, which include self-affirmation, self-preservation, and
aggression. This first formulation was based on the qualitative dis-

tinction between love (preservation of the species) and hunger (self-preservation). In this view human duality is seen as the conflict between that instinct "which strives after objects" and whose chief function is the preservation of the species and that other group of instincts "which aim at preserving the individual" (the ego instincts).[8]

The distinction between sex and ego instincts was reinforced for Freud by the biological distinction between sexuality, which—being aimed at the preservation of the species—has a transpersonal function, and the other biological functions, which aim at the welfare of the individual. This allowed him to see the relationship between the ego and sexuality in two ways: "in the one, the individual is regarded as of prime importance, sexuality as one of his activities and sexual satisfaction as one of his needs; while in the other the individual organism is looked upon as a transitory and perishable appendage to the quasi-immortal germ-plasm bequeathed to him by the race."[9]

Sexuality, according to this description, is ambiguous: on the one hand it is dominated by the ego in seeking personal gratification; on the other hand it serves an altruistic, self-transcending purpose—love and procreation. Hence the ambivalence of love and hate in human relationships. Freud's theoretical explanation was that such ambivalence existed to the extent that the sex instinct was dominated by the ego instincts through failure to outgrow earlier stages of sexuality. The stages of sexual development proper to childhood—the oral, anal, and phallic stages—are egoistic and auto-erotic. Sexual pleasure is derived through the stimulation of the "erogenous zones" of one's own body. It is only with the advent of puberty that mature "genital" sexuality begins to develop. Genital sexuality, being directed towards love objects outside of the self, is altruistic and procreative. Fixation at one of the earlier, immature stages keeps the sex instinct to some extent under the domination of the ego instincts. Fixation at the oral stage, for example, gives sexuality a possessive quality, while fixation at the anal stage imparts qualities of mastery and domination to the sexual aim. "This admixture of hate in love," Freud maintains, "is to be traced in part to those preliminary stages of love which have not been wholly outgrown . . . . the admixture of hate may be traced to the source of the self-preservation instincts."[10]

The publication of Freud's essay "On Narcissism" in 1914

was the occasion for a reformulation of the instinct theory. The concept of narcissism—"an original libidinal cathexis of the ego"[11]—paved the way for the hypothesis of an undifferentiated libido based not on the qualitative difference between love and hunger but on differences in the cathexes of the libido. Now the term "libido" does not refer exclusively to the energy of the sex instinct but to a kind of undifferentiated psychic energy, similar to the meaning given to it by Jung. Human duality, therefore, was no longer a matter of qualitatively different instincts in conflict but rather a conflict resulting from the differences in objects to which the libido might attach itself, namely, the self (ego libido) and love objects external to the self (object libido). This tension between narcissism and object love was seen as a permanent state of affairs since the original infantile narcissism is never fully outgrown. "The ego," Freud maintained, "is the libido's original home and remains to some extent its headquarters" (*CD*, p. 65).

To say, however, that the libido was narcissistic as well as directed towards external objects did not really convey the instinctual dualism to which Freud seemed committed; for it posited a conflict of objects of instinctual impulses rather than a conflict of qualitatively different impulses. In spite of the discovery of narcissism, Freud was not able to give up this commitment to dualism. "Nevertheless," he said, "there still remained in me a kind of conviction, for which I was not as yet able to find reasons, that the instincts could not all be of the same kind" (*CD*, p. 65). It was this conviction which led Freud to return to a dualistic conception of instinctual life. In this third formulation of his instinct theory the duality of human existence consists in the conflict between the life instinct (Eros) and the death instinct. We shall return to this point later, but it is worth noting here that those who smugly dismiss the concept of the death instinct as "unscientific" usually fail to acknowledge that Freud himself did not pretend to offer scientific proof but put it forth as more of an intuitive conviction than a rational conclusion—a conviction for which he was "not as yet able to find reasons." Notice how tentative his language is in enunciating this concept. "After long doubts and vacillations," he writes, "we have decided to assume the existence of only two basic instincts, Eros and the destructive instinct."[12]

This final formulation of instinctual dualism laid bare the inadequacies of the previous formulations. In the first place, both the self-preservative instincts and ego libido were seen as narcissistic forms of love or Eros and did not represent a real contrast to Eros, which included them. In Freud's words, "the contrast between the instincts of self-preservation and the preservation of the species, as well as the contrast between ego love and object love fall within the bounds of Eros."[13] In other words, the previous formulations were not sufficiently radical. To preserve a dualistic and conflictual model it was necessary to discover the real antithesis of Eros. That proved to be the instinct whose aim was not self-preservation but self-destruction. Moreover, the antithesis of Eros and the death instinct is a duality unmitigated by any relationship to the pleasure principle. In the first formulation, the sex and ego instincts were both seen as manifesting the conservative tendency of instinctual life, which Freud described as "an urge inherent in organic life to restore an earlier state of things,"[14] namely, a tensionless state of quiescence. Ungratified instinctual impulses create a state of tension; the aim of the instinctual impulse is to reduce this tension and achieve a tensionless state (homeostasis). In formulating the concept of a death instinct which operates "beyond the pleasure principle" Freud was postulating that the ultimate goal of this conservative tendency of instinctual life was to restore the organism to an ultimate tensionless, inorganic state; that is, to death. If this is the goal of all instinctual life, including Eros, conceived of as the sex instinct, then, according to this earlier formulation, Freud could say that "the aim of life is death."

In the final formulation of the instinct theory, however, Eros is no longer a drive which manifests the conservative nature of instinctual life, but one which, as the antithesis of death, opposes it. In other words, Eros is not simply identical with sexual libido, which operates along with the death instinct according to the conservative nirvana principle. It is now understood as a unifying principle operative in human existence. In his final *Outline of Psychoanalysis* (1940) Freud speaks of Eros as an exception to the conservative character of the instincts:

> If we suppose that living things appeared later than
> inanimate ones and arose out of them, then the death
> instinct agrees with the formula that we have stated,
> to the effect that instincts tend towards a return to
> an earlier state. We are unable to apply the formula

to Eros (the love instinct). That would be to imply
that living substance had once been a unity but had
subsequently been torn apart and was now tending
toward reunion.[15]

I would suggest that it is only by understanding Eros as operating
outside the conservative tendencies of instinctual life or "beyond
the nirvana principle" that we can understand the fundamental
distinction between the death instinct as a divisive principle and
Eros as a unifying principle.

The function of the death instinct is, biologically, to dissolve
the unity of the multicellular organism so that it returns to its inorganic state, and psychologically, to dissolve the unity between individuals through mechanisms of self-affirmation and aggression, as
when, for example, sexuality is dominated by the ego instincts.
Eros is, on the other hand, a unifying force. Biologically it is represented by the tendency of cells to unite in order to form a living
organism. Psychologically it is manifested in the sex instinct which
unites two people in a psychological unity and assures the continu-
ance of the life of the species. The function of Eros, the life instinct,
is to join units of life into ever larger unities, and, as we shall see,
its ultimate goal is "the unity of mankind." It is opposed by the
divisive death instinct, and it is this dualism of Eros and death which
ultimately explains, in Freud's view, the conflicts of human
existence:

> I drew the conclusion that besides the instinct to pre-
> serve living substance and to join it into ever larger
> units, there must exist another, contrary instinct seek-
> ing to dissolve those units and to bring them back to
> their primaeval, inorganic state. That is to say, as well
> as Eros there was an instinct of death. (*CD*, pp. 65–66)

The Theory of Culture

The theory of instincts is the first part of Freud's answer to the
question: Why is there repression? The other part of his answer
is contained in his theory of culture or civilization.[16] In Freudian
theory both the individual and society are explained in terms of
repression. In the words of Norman O. Brown, "in the new

Freudian perspective, the essence of society is repression, and the essence of the individual is repression of himself.''[17] In the conflict between the pleasure principle and the reality principle there are three features of reality which tend to rob the individual of happiness: the forces of nature, biological decay, and human relationships (*CD*, p. 33). The ultimate human response to the first two of these obstacles to happiness is resignation. But the unhappiness that results from our human relationships is another matter. What mars human relationships is the aggressive instinct—''the hostility of each against all and of all against each'' (*CD*, p. 69). In this case, the religious and cultural systems of civilizations try to minimize the effect of human aggressiveness through the control and regulation of interpersonal life.

Aggressiveness, however, is described by Freud as the ''derivative and main representative of the death instinct'' (*CD*, p. 69). It is the death instinct, therefore, turned against others in the form of aggression—a primary masochism turned into sadism ''under the influence of the narcissistic libido''[18]—which destroys the possiblity of happiness in human relationships and accounts for the ''social sources of distress.'' If the essence of society is the repression of the individual, it is because the religious and cultural systems of civilization have as their function the regulating of interpersonal life through the repression of human aggressiveness, which is in turn a manifestation of the death instinct.

The conflict, therefore, between the individual and society is merely a reflection of the instinctual conflict within the individual between Eros and death, and out of this conflict, in Freud's view, civilization is born. ''This struggle,'' he says, ''is what all life essentially consists of, and the evolution of civilization may therefore be simply described as the struggle for life of the human species'' (*CD*, p. 69). This is the ultimate meaning of civilization and the ultimate explanation for the repressions it carries out against the individual. These repressions do not originate in the demands for instinctual renunciation imposed on the individual by civilization. Civilization is created by communities of individuals in order to carry out that repression which is necessary because of the conditions of their individual human natures. Death in the form of aggression must be repressed not merely because of the opposition of civilization but ultimately because of the opposition of a conflicting tendency within the individual—the drive towards life.

By thus repressing the death instinct in the form of aggression, the cultural, religious, and social institutions of civilization
attempt to create the conditions necessary for the ultimate triumph
of life over death. In this way, civilization serves Eros' goal of unity
by repressing the divisive force of the death instinct. Notice that
Freud does not say that Eros serves the ends of civilization but that
"civilization is a process in the service of Eros whose purpose is
to combine single human individuals, and after that families, then
races, peoples and nations into one great unity, the unity of mankind" (CD, p. 69). In the words of Paul Ricoeur, "culture comes
upon the scene as the great enterprise of making life prevail against
death."[19] This enterprise is twofold. It consists of the sublimation
of sexuality and the repression of aggressiveness.

The mere repression of aggressive tendencies is not sufficient
for the building up of civilized society and the ultimate triumph
of Eros. If individuals are to live together in community, they must
be bound together by ties of friendship; in Freud's words, they must
be "libidinally bound" to one another. "Necessity alone," he
argues, "the advantages of life in common, will not hold them
together" (CD, p. 69). In other words, rational, utilitarian motives
will not of themselves compel us to behave justly and morally
towards one another; what is needed is an affective bond. This
means that the libido—the energy of the life instinct—is to be
directed towards other than strictly sexual objects. Hence civilization puts restrictions on sexual love, channelling it into genital,
heterosexual, and monogamous expressions, and directing the surplus "desexualized" energy towards cultural pursuits (sublimation)
and "aim-inhibited" love or friendship, thus establishing a bond
among people which runs contrary to their natural aggressive
instincts (CD, pp. 58–59).

The thwarting and sublimating of erotic desire produces civilized man's well-known neurotic symptoms, while the repression
of the aggressive instinct produces a heightened sense of guilt. Hence
the central theme of Civilization and Its Discontents is that "the price
of progress in civilization is paid in forfeiting happiness through
heightening the sense of guilt" (CD, p. 81). Under the influence
of civilization, aggressiveness, which is the externalized expression
of the death instinct, is once again internalized, but this time in
the form of guilt since the energy of the repressed aggressiveness
is appropriated by the superego and turned against one's own ego.

The death instinct is now experienced in the form of guilt and the need for punishment (*CD*, pp. 70–71). Hence the crucial nature of the Oedipus complex for the process of civilization, for it is at this stage that, under the extraneous authority of culture represented by the parental figure, the child's sexual drive becomes aim-inhibited or "desexualized" and his aggressive drive is repressed through the process of internalizing the parental authority.

For Freud, the developmental task of the Oedipal phase of childhood (age four to five) is the successful resolution of the Oedipus complex—that complex of feelings which Freud ascribed to the male child at this stage towards his parents: attraction to the mother as an object of sexual love, and ambivalent feelings of love and hostility towards the father as a rival for the mother's love. In Freud's view, when this complex is successfully resolved, two things happen: the child renounces the mother as sexual object, and his love for her becomes "aim-inhibited," tender affection; secondly, the little boy identifies with the father, confirming his masculinity and introjecting or internalizing the commands and prohibitions of the father. The result of such introjection is the formation of the superego and the beginnings of conscience. In this way the child is able to overcome the hostility he feels towards his father as the obstacle to his wishes by transferring the source of prohibitions and obstacles to instinctual impulses from an external source (the father) to an internal source (the superego).[20]

This internalizing of the authority of the father is the beginning of the process of internalizing civilization's cultural prohibitions, for in this instance the father represents the extraneous authority of culture, which decides what is good and bad. As the child grows, the same internalizing of authority will take place in wider forms of communal life beyond the family. Thus the "loss of happiness through heightening the sense of guilt," which Freud sees as the price of such internalizing of authority, is continually reinforced. It is the unifying life instinct which impels us to identify with ever larger groups—social, occupational, religious, ethnic, etc. In doing so, we internalize the social and moral standards of the group, and it is precisely because we have internalized those standards—made them our own—that we experience guilt or a lack of integrity as a result of our failure to conform to them. The contradiction inherent, therefore, in the process of civilization is that Eros can only achieve its goal of unity through a continual reinforcing of that sense

of guilt which we first experienced in relation to the authority of
the parental figure. "What began in relation to the father," says
Freud, "is completed in relation to the group" (CD, p. 80).

Two points should be noted in passing about the process of
internalization. In the first place, it involves the repression of the
individual's aggressiveness towards the authority represented by
society as such. It is the energy of this aggressiveness which Freud
believed was appropriated by the superego and directed towards
oneself. If we accept Freud's premise that aggression is an externalized expression of the death instinct, then one of the results of
the process of civilization and socialization is that the death instinct
is once again internalized and experienced in the form of guilt.
Secondly, we must avoid the temptation of interpreting Freud's
views in such a way as to make them conform to those of contemporary "pop psychologists," who seem intent on offering us the
possibility of a life free of guilt, anxiety, and discontent. As we have
seen, Freud's view of the human condition is essentially tragic.
Hence, when he speaks of the process of socialization, internalization, and the guilt which results from this process, he is not speaking
of some neurotic aberration but of the price that must be paid for
the benefits of civilization. In *The Future of an Illusion* he speaks of
the moral sense which results from the internalizing of civilization's
cultural prohibitions as one of the "mental assets" of civilization.
It is through this process, he notes, "that external coercion gradually becomes internalized; for a special mental agency, man's superego, takes it over and includes it among its commandments."[21]
It is through this process, he argues, that we become moral and
social beings and are turned from being opponents of civilization
into being its vehicles. The more successful this process is, the more
culture can dispense with external coercion. For these reasons he
regards the strengthening of the superego as "a most precious
cultural asset in the psychological field."[22]

Can Life Prevail? The Psychoanalytic Response

The picture of the human condition which emerges from Freudian
theory is pessimistic because, in delineating the tragic dimension
of human existence, it offers little hope. If the basis of civilization

is instinctual renunciation by the individual in the interests of communal life, then a tension is set up between civilization and its values and the demands of individual life. The result is a reversal of the individual's priorities. Whereas the individual's goals are primarily egoistic (his own happiness) and secondarily altruistic (merging with others), the goals of culture are primarily communal (unification according to the life instinct) and only secondarily the happiness of the individual. Civilization thus reverses the individual's priorities; and this is the most obvious reason for the civilized person's "discontent." "If civilization," Freud argues, "imposes such great sacrifices not only on man's sexuality but on his aggressivity, we can understand better why it is hard for him to be happy in that civilization" (*CD*, p. 62). Freud points out that the desire to escape from these restrictions, which expresses itself as the desire for freedom, may take the form of a revolt against the injustice of a particular form of civilization and demand changes that contribute to the progress of civilization. One of the problems facing modern democratic societies is how to find a balance between such legitimate forms of dissent (e.g., anti-nuclear groups, the women's movement, environmentalists) and the equally legitimate demands of society as a whole; for dissent can also take the form of anarchy. It may constitute a revolt against civilization itself, in which case it originates in "the remains of . . . original personality, which is still untamed by civilization" (*CD*, p. 43).

Freud is not optimistic about the possibility of finding a particular form of civilization which represents "an expedient accommodation . . . between this claim of the individual and the cultural claims of the group" (*CD*, p. 43). Unlike Herbert Marcuse, his vision is not that of a "non-repressive civilization" but of a civilization that will continue to demand the repression of the aggressiveness of our original untamed personality. The reason for this, as we have seen, is that the ultimate source of repression is not civilization but the biologically rooted dualism of our human nature. Since we cannot change our human nature, we are condemned to live with a certain measure of unhappiness or discontent due to the sublimation of our erotic impulses, which turns our goals into substitute goals, and to the sense of guilt which results from the internalizing of the aggressive instincts. For Freud, the process of civilization was, in the end, self-defeating. It begins as an attempt to create the conditions necessary for the triumph of life (Eros) over death. In order to make Eros triumph it represses the death instinct in the form of aggression; but the energy of the internalized aggression is appropriated by the superego and directed towards oneself. Thus the death instinct continues to dominate human existence in the form of guilt. In the words of Paul Ricoeur, "civilization kills us to make us live."[23]

In the face of this analysis of the tragic dimensions of human existence, later interpreters of Freud within the psychoanalytic tradition have engaged in what is essentially a religious enterprise, attempting to find a "way out" of Freud's pessimism and offer hope in the midst of tragedy. Frequently this involves a fundamental revision of Freudian theory, a denial of the reality of the death instinct and/or the biologically rooted dualism of human nature. This kind of revision is sometimes represented as an attempt to develop the "radical" dimension of Freud's theory, but ends precisely in a denial of its most radical feature.

Erich Fromm, for example, attempts to liberate psychoanalysis from what he considers Freud's conservative and conformist tendencies, which allegedly explain his acceptance of the inevitability and necessity of cultural repression and therefore of a therapy which aims at adjustment to the prevailing cultural milieu.[24] In order to make Freudian theory a more radical vehicle for social criticism it is necessary for Fromm to find the sources of repression in social environment and institutions rather than in human nature itself. Freud had located the source of repression in the struggle between Eros and the death instinct. Fromm begins by dismissing the concept of the death instinct as "an unproved speculation" based on the hypothesis of the repetition compulsion.[25] But, as we have noted already, Freud, while he looked for evidence for his hypothesis, never advanced the concept of the death instinct as a logical or scientific conclusion. In speaking of his ideas on the fundamental duality of Eros and the death instinct, he states that he originally advanced these ideas tentatively but admits that in the course of time "they have gained such a hold upon me that I can no longer think in any other way" (CD, p. 66). I would suggest that just as Freud himself held this view on more than scientific grounds, those who reject the concept of the death instinct also do so on more than scientific grounds. Perhaps the real reason for this rejection is that the concept of the death instinct results in a pessimistic view of the human condition and a modification of the Eros/death dualism is the only theoretical way out of that pessimism.

Fromm rejects the biological dualism of life and death, in which the positive and negative forces have equal strength, and replaces it with a dualism in which the life force ("biophilia"— the love of life) is primary and the destructive force ("necrophilia"— the love of death) is reduced to the status of a "secondary potentiality." The love of death only becomes operative when and to the extent that the love of life is blocked from developing by social or environmental conditions.[26] Destructiveness is not an inherent instinct but "the outcome of unlived life."[27] The normal thrust of human growth, therefore, is in the direction of biophilia, while necrophilia is a pathological result of unfavourable environmental conditions. Moreover, the distinction between biophilia and necrophilia is not a distinction between biologically rooted instincts but between opposing "character orientations." They are merely potentialities which depend for their development on social conditioning. This is a more "radical" view of the human condition only in the sense that it makes room for a more radical critique of social systems and institutions. But the Freudian view remains a more radical view of human existence since it locates the source of human discontent within individual human nature rather than in the environment. Fromm's "humanistic psychoanalysis" shares with humanistic thought in general the concept of a human nature which is naturally good. If such is the case, the source of evil and destructiveness is in the environment, and the answer to the problem is in the restructuring of that environment—of our social and cultural institutions—through social revolution. But if the ultimate source of evil and destructiveness lies within human nature itself, as Freud believed, then we must either yield to Freud's pessimism or have recourse to a religious answer and look to some transcendent source of redemption and healing.

Unlike Fromm, Herbert Marcuse accepts the duality of Eros and death, but the basis of the hope he offers is his contention that this instinctual duality is historical rather than biological in origin. In his *Eros and Civilization* he argues that the purpose of the psychoanalytic technique of recalling the past is not reconciliation with present reality but the rediscovery of the truth of the pleasure principle, which the repressive force of civilization has relegated to the unconscious. What we desire, he maintains, is a restoration of the repressed Eros, and this "return of the repressed" is an essentially religious quest—the desire to regain a paradise lost. Civilization labels this desire as pathological and represses it in favour of the reality principle. Marcuse aruges that for the sake of power and domination, social institutions carry this repression of Eros beyond what is indispensable for civilized human association. This "surplus repression" of erotic impulses produces the Eros/death conflict, which is historical in origin and not rooted in human nature. For Marcuse, the death instinct represents a flight from the pain and repression which result from historically conditioned social conditions. The answer, therefore, to the problems created by civilization is the strengthening of Eros through the removal of surplus repression.

The Eros/death antagonism is, therefore, of historical origin. Biologically, Marcuse argues for an original unity of Eros and death, each being manifestations of the nirvana principle, the striving for quiescence and the absence of tension. As we have seen, in the final formulation of his instinct theory, Freud attributed such a conservative tendency only to the death instinct, whose aim was to return to an original inorganic state. He could find no evidence for an original unity, the recapturing of which would be the object of the life instinct. As we have also seen, this was so because he had considerably refined the concept of Eros, so that it no longer shared with the death instinct the conservative aim of the nirvana principle but opposed it. It is only by equating Eros with sexuality that Marcuse is able to posit an original unity of Eros and death on the basis that both manifest the nirvana principle. Consequently he can argue that the antagonism of Eros and death is historically acquired—the disruption of an original harmony; and that the solution of this duality lies in the strengthening of the repressed Eros through the elimination of surplus repression.

For Marcuse, therefore, our hope lies in the possibility of a "non-repressive civilization" in which the removal of surplus repression would permit the "self-sublimation" of Eros. In other words, if erotic impulses are allowed free expression, they will seek, without the need of repression, those non-sexual, libidinal ties with others which Freud saw as the basis of civilization. In Marcuse's words, "the biological drive becomes a cultural drive,"[28] and this strengthening rather than weakening of Eros is the force which counteracts the destructive instinct. "The culture building power of Eros," he states, "is non-repressive sublimation: sexuality is neither deflected from nor blocked in its objective; rather in attaining its objective, it transcends it to others, searching for fuller gratification."[29]

Again, it would seem, a way has been found to overcome Freudian pessimism by locating the source of duality and conflict in the historical cultural process rather than in human nature itself. Marcuse's optimism, however, is arrived at by distorting the basic meaning of certain Freudian concepts, particularly the concept of Eros. Erich Fromm takes Marcuse to task for not basing his philosophical speculations on the clinical data which is the basis of psychoanalysis. This causes him, Fromm argues, to distort the meaning of Freudian concepts such as the pleasure principle, the reality principle, repression, and Eros. He points out that, in attributing the same conservative nature to Eros as to the death instinct, Marcuse "is apparently unaware that after some wavering Freud arrived, in the *Outline of Psychoanalysis*, at the opposite conclusion, namely that Eros does not partake of the conservative nature."[30] In the end he describes the ideal of Marcuse's non-repressive society as "an infantile paradise where all work is play and where there is no serious conflict or tragedy."[31]

Norman O. Brown is perhaps the most radical of Freud's interpreters since he is closer to Freud's own radicalism. He agrees with Marcuse that the source of human discontent is the repression of infantile sexuality through the genital organization imposed by the reality principle, and that our essential desire pertains to recapturing in some way the life of childhood—a life governed by the pleasure principle. Civilization offers us substitute satisfactions but "man remains unconvinced because in infancy he tasted the fruit of the tree of life, and knows that it is good, and never forgets."[32] Again, as with Marcuse, he posits an original unity of instinctual impulses in which the instincts are not antagonistic but compatible with each other. Hence the human person need not be condemned to instinctual dualism and repression. This original unity refers to the fact that, under the influence of primary narcissism, the original ego feeling embraced the whole world, creating a unity of self and world, of ego libido and object libido. This primal condition is typified in the relation of the child to the mother's breast, in which the satisfaction of hunger (narcissism) and the satisfaction of love (union with an object) are accomplished in the same act. The goal of human striving, he contends, is the overcoming of dualism and the recovery of this primal state.

Brown's understanding of the Eros/death duality, however, is closer to Freud's own formulation than to either Fromm's or Marcuse's. Unlike Fromm, he does not reduce the death instinct to a mere "secondary potentiality"; unlike Marcuse, he recognizes Freud's refined understanding of Eros as "a desire for union (being one) with objects in the world."[33] Consequently, he is less inclined to see any hope for humanity in the possibility of a triumph of Eros over death. Rather what he looks for is a reunion or refusion of life and death—the restoration of an original instinctual unity— and finds Freud's description of an organizing and synthesizing ego seeking ever wider unities, and thereby achieving a sort of victory of Eros over death, as too optimistic.[34] The pursuit of this goal, which is in reality a flight from death, is, in Brown's view, the source of human discontent.

     We are restless, Brown argues, because we cannot accept death, which is therefore in an antagonistic relationship to the forces of life. Such an antagonism does not exist in the animal world, where the instincts exist in a condition of undifferentiated unity or harmony. Repression and therefore neurosis exist only at the human level of life and are not biological necessities. Only at the human level of life are the polarities of Eros and death separated. For at this level of life the nirvana principle, which at the animal level represents the aim of life in general, becomes identified with the death instinct and is thereby divorced from the pleasure principle, which represents the tendency of Eros, a restless pursuit of pleasure which repression denies us. "To identify the pleasure principle with man," Brown states, "and the nirvana principle with life in general is only another way of saying that man and only man is the neurotic animal."[35] Also, at the human level of life, the repetition compulsion is divorced from the pleasure principle; that is, it is no longer a desire for pleasurable repetition but a regressive fixation to the past. And lastly there exists an ambivalent relationship between Eros and death since the death instinct is externalized in the form of aggression. Brown argues that this extroverted death instinct is a way of solving the life-death conflict at the human level which does not exist at the biological level. It represents, therefore, a "flight from death" because we fear the separation and individuality which is the aim of the death instinct.

     In Brown's view, our only hope lies in the possibility of an unrepressed life—a life which leaves no "unlived lines"—for in such a life the body is willing to die, the death instinct is affirmed, and Eros and death are reconciled. The removal of repression makes possible a return to a more natural state and an end to the restless pursuit of society's substitute satisfactions and the neurotic flight from death. An unrepressed life lets Eros seek its goal of union while allowing death to maintain separateness. In the midst of tragedy, therefore, Brown offers hope in the form of a reconciliation of the forces of life and death: "The possibility of redemption lies in the reunification of the instinctual opposites."[36] In such reunification "the primal unity Eros seeks to reinstate is its unity with its opposite, the death instinct."[37]

We have been seeking the psychoanalytic response to the question "Can life prevail over death?" and we have seen that the response is varied. Both Freud and Fromm look to the possibility of restructuring civilization's social and cultural institutions in such a way as to promote the victory of the life forces over death. As we have seen, however, Freud does so with considerably less optimism than Fromm since he sees the source of death as originating in human nature itself rather than in social structures. Marcuse and Brown look for a solution to the human dilemma in the recapturing of an original unity which precedes either historically or biologically the instinctual dualism which besets human existence. The speculations of these four psychoanalytic thinkers remind us that the question underlying the religious enterprise of offering hope in the midst of tragedy is twofold: (1) What is the source of the tragic quality of human existence and how is that tragic quality to be overcome? (2) Is the basis of human hope to be found in a regressive movement which tries to recapture an earlier state of affairs (a paradise lost), or are we to hope for a new level of existence to be achieved in the future? Does human salvation consist in the "return of the repressed" or the arrival of something new? The psychoanalytic concepts of repression, sublimation, and substitute gratification suggest the concept of a more natural state of existence preceding or apart from civilization's repressions and to which we desire to return. Such a concept correlates with the idea that the human religious sentiment—the desire for self-transcendence—has its origin in a certain nostalgia for a paradise lost. Erik Erikson describes the process of the disruption of the child's original oneness with the mother as resulting in a lifelong sense of being deprived, of being divided (as the result of growing self-awareness), and of being abandoned.[38] The child indeed has a nostalgia for a "paradise lost," which is a psychological analogue to the biblical story of the fall. We shall return to this theme, but it is worth noting that Christianity makes use of both types of imagery. Salvation is the restoration of something that had been lost—the restoration or re-establishing of "all things in Christ" (Eph. 1: 10); at the same time it is the creation of something new—a "new life" and a "new creation."

Can Life Prevail? The Christian Response

We have seen that Freud's view of the human condition is tragic and pessimistic. We have also suggested that some neo-Freudians have responded to Freud's pessimism by fundamentally revising his theory in an attempt to find a way out of that pessimism. In *Freud and Man's Soul* Bruno Bettelheim has reacted strongly to this attempt on the part of some of Freud's interpreters to turn Freud's pessimistic and tragic view of life into a "pragmatic meliorism":

> By selectively accepting only some of Freud's ideas
> about the role of the sexual drives in man's makeup,
> and by misunderstanding his tragic belief that man's
> destructive tendencies spring from a dark side of the
> soul, and perverting this belief into a facile theory that
> the negative aspects of man's behaviour are merely
> the consequences of his living in a bad society, many
> of Freud's followers have transformed psychoanalysis
> from a profound view of man's condition into some-
> thing shallow.[39]

As we have seen, Freud saw guilt and discontent as the inevitable price we had to pay for civilization—inevitable because the cause lies ultimately within ourselves—and the paying of this price as much preferable to the alternative, which was to live at the mercy of our destructive impulses. Bettelheim is critical of those inter-preters of *Civilization and Its Discontents* who leave readers with the impression that Freud was critical of civilization and saw it as the cause of human discontent. The readers of such accounts "might imagine that they could have a civilization without discontent, mis-takenly believing that psychoanalysis suggests this is possible and even desirable. Such a notion is childish and narcissistic, completely contrary to what Freud had in mind."[40]

In turning to the Christian response to Freudian pessimism, it should be noted in the first place that it offers humanity a transcendent source of hope in the ultimate triumph of life over death. What I want to suggest, however, is that this recourse to a transcendent source of hope is not just a *deus ex machina*, but the logical consequence of an essential agreement between the Christian and Freudian views of the tragic dimension of human existence. When psychoanalysis first appeared on the scene, a typical Christian judgement was that while psychoanalysis was useful as a therapeutic technique, the fundamental concepts of psychoanalytic theory were at odds with Christian doctrine. Today this judgement is in the process of being reversed, for while the value of psychoanalytic therapy is being questioned, the Freudian analysis of the human condition can be seen as being in fundamental agreement with Christian theological anthropology. This perhaps helps to validate Freud's own contention that the cultural and human significance of psychoanalysis was more important than its medical significance.[41]

The premise of any religion of hope and salvation is the tragic nature of human existence. Consequently, Christianity, unlike the revisions and interpretations we have been discussing, does not fundamentally revise Freud's theory in order to offer hope in the midst of tragedy. With Freud, it finds no real basis for such hope in the human condition and appeals to a source of hope which transcends the possibilities of human nature and human civilization. If, as we have suggested, tragedy is the precondition of hope, then the process of civilization, which brings us to a state of frustration and discontent, constitutes the "boundary situation" in which faith becomes possible; like "the law" for St. Paul, it provides the context in which we become painfully aware of our finitude, our guilt, and our need for redemption. Freud describes civilization as a self-defeating process which tries to promote the triumph of Eros but does so by reinforcing the death instinct in the form of guilt. Perhaps we can find in this description a psychological analysis of transcendence in the Tillichian sense of the tendency of the finite to "point beyond itself." If human civilization's struggle for life ends in the experience of death, then the human striving for life can only be satisfied by a transcendent source. Only faith, however, can posit the existence of such a transcendent source of hope and life.

Since Freud could not answer the question posed by the Eros-death conflict from the perspective of such a faith, his vision of the possibilities of human nature and human civilization remained pessimistic. Nevertheless, his analysis of this tragic dimension of human existence fulfills the definition of what we have called a new style of natural theology for it correlates with and helps to make meaningful the Christian understanding of the fall and redemption. Both Freudian and Christian perceptions of human civilization agree that it cannot achieve its purpose, and—in the Christian view— stands in need of redemption. The point I want to make is that, as far as the possibilities of human nature and human civilization are concerned, Christian anthropology shares Freud's pessimism and finds an answer to that pessimism only in its optimistic theology. If we assume for the moment a point we shall return to shortly— the identification of that "life" which is the object of Christian hope with the Freudian understanding of Eros—we can discover at least three features of the process by which Christian hope is realized which illustrate its consistency with Freudian theory: it is a process which is *historical, paradoxical*, and *redemptive*.

It is historical because life in both the Freudian and Christian sense cannot be understood apart from the historical process of civilization. To say that Christianity is an historical religion as distinct from a religion of nature is to say that the object of Christian hope—the "kingdom of God"—is the end result of the historical process even though it is a transcendent goal which depends on divine intervention for its realization, and is not simply the actualization of the potentialities inherent in man and his cultural institutions. Thus, the Christian paraphrase of Freud's definition of civilization—"a process in the service of Eros"—would define civilization as "a process in the service of the kingdom." The concepts of Eros and the kingdom of God have a similar function, to give meaning and purpose to civilization and the historical process. While both Herbert Marcuse and Norman O. Brown seem to want to stop the historical process—to cancel time—in order to return to a primal state of instinctual gratification, Freud, in spite of the theoretical difficulties involved, tried to give meaning to history.

Ultimately, he failed because he could find no way out of the contradiction inherent in a civilization which, in order to promote Eros, had to inflict death, in the form of guilt, on its members. If Christianity continues in spite of this contradiction to hope for an ultimate triumph of life over death, it is by reason of an assurance of faith based on a belief in Christ's victory over death. The kingdom of God—the triumph of life over death—represents the transcendent goal of civilization, a goal which transcends the possibilities of civilization and its repressions.

Secondly, the process of realizing hope is paradoxical. We have seen that for Freud the process of civilization reverses the individual's priorities, subordinating his egoistic desire for personal happiness to the altruistic goal of creating community, thus creating the conditions for his discontent. Christianity turns this contradiction into a paradox by offering personal fulfillment and happiness to the person who renounces such an egoistic goal in favour of the goal of community, who "loses" his life in order to "find" it (Matt. 8:39). Gabriel Marcel expresses the same paradox in arguing that the basis for hope in individual immortality is to be found, not in some quality of individual life such as an immortal soul, but rather in the capacity of the individual to transcend himself and establish bonds of love with his fellow human beings. In his reflections on "Death and Hope" in *The Mystery of Being*, he contends that hope for immortality is not to be found in the "noumenal," that is, in the fact that one possesses an immortal soul which survives the death of the body. That which resists death is not any quality inherent in individual human nature but rather the bond of love which unites individuals. "It is not, I think, from the noumenal point of view that the indestructibility of the loved being can be affirmed: the indestructibility is much more that of a bond than that of an object."[42] In Marcel's view it is only by transcending one's isolated ego striving and entering into that intersubjective and communal life which, as we have seen, is the goal of Eros that one can have any "prophetic assurance" of immortality. "What is really important," he states, "is the destiny of that living link, and not that of an entity which is isolated and closed in upon itself."[43]

This self-transcending power of interpersonal life resisting the death wish of the isolated individual is precisely the meaning which Paul Ricoeur, interpreting Freud, assigns to Eros:

> If the living substance goes to death by an inner movement, what fights against death is not something internal to life, but the configuration of two mortal substances. Freud calls this configuration Eros: the desire of the other is directly implied in the emergence of

Eros; it is always with another that the living substance fights against death, against its own death, whereas when it acts separately, it pursues death through the circuitous route of adaptation to the natural and cultural environment. Freud does not look for the drive for life in some will to live inscribed in each living substance: in the living substance by itself he finds only death.[44]

The "life" therefore which is the object of Christian hope is essentially interpersonal and communal and therefore consistent with the unifying aim of Eros. Hence the biblical identification of "life" with the "kingdom of God." If the kingdom refers to that unity among people which for the believer is the result of those works of love which spring from faith, and for Freud is a manifestation of the unifying principle of Eros, then even according to Freudian understanding, to be admitted to the kingdom is to "enter into life" (Matt. 17; 19:17; 25:46). If, therefore, we interpret "life" as the unifying principle of Eros, the paradox of losing one's life in order to find it refers to the conviction that true life is to be found only in transcending the pursuit of individual fulfillment in favour of union with the other. Hence the vital connection between life and love.[45]

Thirdly, the process resulting in the triumph of Eros is redemptive. If civilization inevitably fails in its pursuit of Eros, it is, according to Freud, because its existence depends on fostering a sense of guilt in individuals. If a culture based on the life instinct rather than death is a remote possibility, it is because culture's weapon is guilt and, therefore, civilization is ultimately founded on the death instinct. The triumph of Eros over death is made possible, therefore, only through some process of redemption or liberation from guilt. Christianity is historical in that it does not operate apart from the guilt-producing process of civilization described by Freud but redeems it by offering humanity a transcendent source of redemption from its inevitable sense of guilt.

If civilization "kills us to make us live," the death here referred to is occasioned by the internalizing of the destructive death instinct through the formation of the guilt-producing superego. This is our encounter with "the law" which for St. Paul was an instrument of death (guilt), but a death which was a precondition of life

(Rom. 7:9–10). Hence for St. Paul liberation from the law through grace was seen as liberation from death (Rom. 8:2). In the Christian understanding, therefore, there is no escape from the reality principle and the guilt it inflicts. For Paul Ricoeur, religion is both the abandonment of desire and the fulfillment of desire.[46] Though it may be originally motivated by the desire to recapture what has been lost, a nostalgia for a paradise lost, that past is not recaptured by a simple regression to some primal unrepressed state but by a rebirth to something new. The past is not recaptured by clinging to it but by renouncing it in favour of the future—even though that future inevitably holds out the prospect of death—for tragedy is a precondition of hope and death is a precondition of life. In the Old Testament God's saving will is portrayed in the story of Yahweh leading his people to the promised land but by way of the hardships of the desert, and in the New Testament by the image of Christ resolutely turning his face towards Jerusalem and the cross that awaited him.

I have suggested that there is a fundamental agreement between the Freudian and Christian analyses of the human condition. Both identify the source of human guilt and discontent as a duality or conflict which is inherent in individual human nature. Freudian theory identifies the poles of the intrasubjective dualism as the life instinct (Eros) and the death instinct; Christianity speaks of the conflict in terms of "life," which is the object of the believer's hope, and "sin," which is the obstacle to the realization of that hope. In comparing these concepts we have observed a parallel between Eros and the life which is the object of Christian hope in that both are conceived of as essentially intersubjective and interpersonal experiences. It is perhaps worth noting in this regard that the New Testament images which describe the fullness of life—the "kingdom of God"—are essentially communal images: the kingdom is variously described as a banquet, a wedding feast, a vine and its branches, a net full of fish, a field in which wheat and weeds grow together. The life of the kingdom is described as the reward of those who have practised the works of love and mercy which promote Eros' goal of unity (Matt. 25:31–46). Images such as the separation of the goats from the sheep, the weeds from the wheat, the good fish from the bad, the unworthy from the worthy wedding guests suggest that the kingdom represents the prefection of a community rather than an individual reward.

Our discussion of the process by which hope is realized has identified, I believe, two further points of similarity between the Freudian Eros and the Christian concept of life. In the first place both are conceived of as the *transcendent* goal of human becoming (that is, the authentic goal of human growth which is nevertheless beyond the capacity of human nature or human civilization to achieve). According to the Freudian analysis we seek Eros, but human efforts end in the experience of death in the form of guilt. Christianity also speaks of the life it promises as being beyond human achievement and possible only through the experience of divine grace. The important point, in the context of our discussion, is that the "life" which Christianity promises is, according to Freudian theory, consistent with the deepest human aspirations. That life, therefore, is not something "tacked on" to human growth and existence; it represents the thrust and goal of authentic human growth. It is, however, the *transcendent* goal of that growth.

Secondly, life in both the Freudian and Christian understanding must be preceded by the experience of "death" as a necessary precondition. The fundamental Christian symbolism is that of crucifixion and resurrection, death and rebirth. One must die in order to live. We have seen, though he was pessimistic on this point, that Freud believed humanity's only hope for the triumph of Eros over death lay not in any regressive attempt to recapture the past but in the forward moving process of civilization even though that process involved the experience of death in the form of guilt. For Christianity also, the path to life is by way of redemption from the inevitable guilt which civilization inflicts upon us, not in the avoidance of that guilt.

Is it possible to find similar parallels between the Freudian concept of the death instinct and the Christian concept of sin? We shall deal with the question of "original sin" more fully in the next chapter. In the meantime it will suffice perhaps to note that both sin and the death instinct are seen as the intrasubjective causes of guilt, anxiety, and discontent. The death instinct is a biologically rooted tendency of individual human nature. Sin, in the traditional Christian view, is "original"—part and parcel of the human condition—and is not caused by any social condition or historical process. As well, both sin and the death instinct manifest themselves in human ego-striving. For Freud, the death instinct externalized itself in the form of the ego instincts—egoism, aggression, self-affirmation, mastery and domination—all of which partake of the divisive character of the death instinct. Thus human acts of egoism find their source in a quality or tendency of human nature itself. This corresponds to the Christian distinction between "sins," individual acts which violate moral principles, and "sin," the basic human condition which is the ultimate source of "sins" or transgressions and which Stanislas Lyonnet describes as "that deeply rooted egoism by whch man, since original sin, orientates everything to himself instead of opening himself to God and to others."[47] Egoistic behaviour, therefore, is the tangible evidence of a reality which dominates human existence. That reality may be described theologically as sin and psychoanalytically as the death instinct.

NOTES

1. Sigmund Freud, *A General Introduction to Psychoanalysis*, trans. Joan Riviere (New York: Washington Square Press, 1952), p. 296.
2. Paul Tillich, *The Shaking of the Foundations* (New York: Scribner's, 1948), pp. 64–75.
3. Paul Tillich, *The Courage to Be* (London: Fontana, 1962), p. 153.
4. Paul Tillich, as quoted in James Luther Adams, *Paul Tillich's Philosophy of Culture, Science and Religion* (New York: Harper and Row, 1965), p. 43.
5. Carl Jung, *Memories, Dreams, Reflections*, trans. Richard and Clara Winston (New York: Random House, 1963), p. 325.
6. William James, *The Varieties of Religious Experience* (New York: Macmillan, 1961), Lectures 6–7.
7. Ibid., p. 119.
8. Sigmund Freud, *Civilization and Its Discontents*, trans. James Strachey (New York: Norton, 1961), p. 64. In this chapter this work is hereafter referred to as *CD*; all further quotations from it are cited in the text.
9. Sigmund Freud, "The Instincts and Their Vicissitudes," in *Collected Papers*, ed. Joan Riviere, 5 vols. (London: Hogarth Press, 1924–1950), 4:68.
10. Ibid., p. 82.
11. Sigmund Freud, "On Narcissism: An Introduction," in *Collected Papers*, 4:33.
12. Sigmund Freud, *An Outline of Psychoanalysis*, trans. James Strachey (New York: Norton, 1949), p. 20.
13. Ibid., p. 20.

14. Sigmund Freud, *Beyond the Pleasure Principle*, trans. James Strachey (New York: Bantam Books, 1967), p. 67.
15. Freud, *An Outline of Psychoanalysis*, pp. 20–21. See also *CD*, p. 65, footnote 2.
16. For Freud, the words *culture* and *civilization* are used interchangeably to denote "the whole sum of achievements and regulations which distinguish our lives from those of our animal ancestors and which serve two purposes—namely to protect men against nature and to adjust their mutual arrangements" (*CD*, p. 36). See also Sigmund Freud, *The Future of an Illusion*, trans. James Strachey (New York: Norton, 1961), pp. 1–2.
17. Norman O. Brown, *Life against Death: The Psychoanalytic Meaning of History* (New York: Random House, 1959) p. 3.
18. Freud, *Beyond the Pleasure Principle*, p. 95.
19. Paul Ricoeur, *Freud and Philosophy: An Essay on Interpretation*, trans. Denis Savage (New Haven: Yale University Press, 1970), p. 309.
20. The obvious bias and one-sidedness of Freud's interpretation of the Oedipus complex (its exclusive application to the male child, the predominant role of the father, and the essentially sexual character of the conflict) have been pointed out by other theorists (e.g., Adler, Jung, Fromm) and should not distract our attention from the essential features of the Oedipal stage which are relevant for our discussion, namely, the processes of identification and of internalizing parental commands and prohibitions which are characteristic of this stage of development and which represent the beginning of the internalizing process which Freud sees as one of the foundations of civilization. For an interesting discussion of Freud's one-sidedness on this point, see Erich Fromm, *The Sane Society* (Greenwich, Conn.: Fawcett Publications, 1955), pp. 42–51.
21. Freud, *The Future of an Illusion*, p. 11.
22. Ibid., p. 11. It should be noted that the formation of the superego is only the beginning of the process of developing a mature conscience, which involves more than obedience to an internalized voice of authority. The internalized commands and prohibitions must be subjected to critical sifting—normally during adolescence—before they can be transformed into one's own moral values.
23. Ricoeur, *Freud and Philosophy*, p. 323.
24. See chapter 1 of Erich Fromm, *The Crisis of Psychoanalysis* (Greenwich, Conn.: Fawcett Publications, 1970).
25. Erich Fromm, *The Heart of Man: Its Genius for Good and Evil* (New York: Harper and Row, 1964), p. 49.
26. See chapter 3 of Fromm, *The Heart of Man*.
27. Erich Fromm, *Man for Himself* (Greenwich Conn.: Fawcett Publications, 1965), p. 216.
28. Herbert Marcuse, *Eros and Civilization: A Philosophical Inquiry into Freud* (Boston: Beacon, 1955), p. 212.

29. Ibid., p. 211. Marcuse's concept of self-sublimation resembles Abraham Maslow's "hierarchy of needs," in which the higher human needs, such as the need for self-actualization, emerge only after the lower needs, such as bodily and sexual needs, have been satisfied.
30. Fromm, *The Crisis of Psychoanalysis*, p. 28.
31. Ibid.
32. Brown, *Life against Death*, p. 31.
33. Ibid., p. 44.
34. Ibid., p. 85. This is an unusual reading of Freudian theory which, while it leaves humanity no other object of hope save the possibility of a victory of Eros over death, is by no means optimistic about such a possibility.
35. Ibid., p. 90.
36. Ibid., p. 86.
37. Ibid., p. 133.
38. Erik Erikson, *Identity and the Life Cycle* (New York: Norton, 1980), pp. 62–63.
39. Bruno Bettelheim, *Freud and Man's Soul* (New York: Knopf, 1983), p. 16.
40. Ibid., p. 101.
41. See lecture 34 in Sigmund Freud, "New Introductory Lectures on Psychoanalysis," in *The Standard Edition of the Complete Psychological Works of Sigmund Freud*, gen. ed. James Strachey, 24 vols. (London: Hogarth Press, 1953–1974), 22:1–182.
42. Gabriel Marcel, *The Mystery of Being II* (Chicago: Regnery, 1965), p. 172.
43. Ibid., p. 174.
44. Ricoeur, *Freud and Philosophy*, p. 291.
45. The concept of self-transcendence is at the heart of Viktor Frankl's therapeutic technique (Logotherapy). Frankl maintains that self-actualization can never be achieved if it is made a conscious goal; it can only take place as a by-product or side-effect of self-transcendence, that is, commitment to a person, task, or cause outside of the self.
46. Ricoeur, *Freud and Philosophy*, p. 275.
47. Stanislas Lyonnet, "St. Paul: Liberty and Law," in *The Bridge: A Yearbook of Judaeo-Christian Studies*, ed. John M. Oesterreicher (New York: Pantheon Books, 1962), 4:237–38.

Chapter 3
Faith and Human Destiny

THE Christian vision of human destiny may be summarized in three doctrinal themes: (1) in its description of human nature as "fallen" and in need of redemption in the doctrine of "original sin"; (2) in its account of how the alienation of the fall is overcome and human nature restored to its essential being in the doctrine of redemption; and (3) in the meaning it gives to the cultural-historical process by defining the ultimate goal of that process as one of eschatological fulfillment. In this chapter I want to suggest that Freudian and psychoanalytic concepts might be helpful in clarifying the meaning of these three doctrinal themes, which are central to Christian thought and which have been the subject of much theological discussion and reinterpretation in recent years.

Original Sin

We have already observed how some interpreters of Freud have tried to avoid the pessimistic conclusions of Freudian theory by revising that theory in such a way as to locate the source of evil and unhappiness in social, historical, or environmental factors rather than in individual human nature. A similar shift has occurred in the thought of some theologians who have replaced the traditional understanding of original sin as a given of individual human nature with the concept of the "sin of the world" which accounts for the inevitability of sin and evil in terms of harmful environmental influences. All such attempts at doctrinal reinterpretation face the challenge of reconciling contemporary insights with traditional doctrinal formulations. For this reason it will be helpful to limit our discussion to the debate about original sin among Catholic theologians, for this debate illustrates the dilemma facing the theologian who, in attempting to make traditional church teaching intelligible and relevant for his or her times, must often work within the framework of a doctrinal formulation which is deeply entrenched in the tradition but suffers all the limitations imposed by the historical and cultural context of its authorship.

Theological reflection on the Catholic doctrine of original sin in recent years has had to face just such a dilemma; namely, how to incorporate contemporary situational, existential, and evolutionary insights into the meaning of the doctrine while remaining faithful to the formula of Trent, which states that original sin is transmitted to the descendants of Adam *propagatione non imitatione*.[1] Because the more obvious implications of this formula, namely the association of sin with the sexual procreative act and the notion of a biological connection of the human race with an historical Adam to account for the universality and inevitability of sin, are unacceptable to the mainstream of contemporary theology, Catholic theologians have attempted to discover the authentic meaning and intent of the Tridentine formula by assigning to the word *generation* (*propagatio*) a wider meaning than mere physical procreation.

André-Marie Dubarle justifies such an attempt at reinterpretation by pointing out that the main point of doctrinal definition of the canons in which the formula appears is the meaning of justification, not the transmission of original sin. The formula of transmission through generation, therefore, does not belong to the strictly defining part of any canon but appears in a relative clause or in a chapter of doctrinal exposition.[2] Therefore, Dubarle concludes, "a certain latitude for theological interpretation remains possible."[3] The purpose of the following remarks will be to examine briefly the theological reinterpretation of the term *generation* in terms of the concept of the "sin of the world"; and to suggest that a psychoanalytic interpretation might be more helpful in clarifying the traditional meaning of the doctrine, and the original intent of the Tridentine formula.

The most obvious intent of the formula *propagatione non imitatione* is that by rejecting the Pelagian doctrine that men are drawn into sin by the example of Adam (i.e., by imitation), it preserves the idea of the universality of sin and of the appropriateness of infant baptism.[4] Such an explanation, however, gives no positive meaning to the term *generation*. In attempting to do so, some Catholic theologians have offered an interpretation which goes beyond the idea of physical generation in a narrow sense. In this view generation refers, not merely to the isolated procreative act, but to the entire process (including both birth and one's ongoing interpersonal relationships) by which each individual enters the human world.[5] But the human world with which one attains solidarity is a sinful world. Original sin, therefore, "is not a static given at birth, but an intrinsically historical dimension of being human in a sinful world," and "grows as our participation in sinful humanity grows."[6]

In such a "situational" view sin is "original" because it is a given, not of individual human nature through physical procreation, but of the situation into which the individual is born and of which he becomes a part. Moreover, his participation in the "sin of the world" is not, in the first instance, a conscious decision (*non imitatione*). Rather, sin works its influence upon the individual before he is able to make responsible moral decisions. Dubarle states:

> Because he comes from a race and an environment
> contaminated by sin, he is himself tainted by this con-
> tagion, which enters his being through all the avenues
> of intrapersonal influence, before he is able to offer
> the least resistance.[7]

It is perhaps true that this situational view gives a more satisfactory account of the involuntary aspect of sin than does the more "personalist" view which appears to be based on the gratuitous assumption that every individual inevitably falls into personal sin. Yet the situational view seems to make an equally gratuitous assumption concerning the inevitability of harmful psychological and social influences. Dubarle, for example, states:

> It is inevitable that there should be some injurious and
> deforming contacts among the multitude of human
> relationships in which a young child becomes involved,
> and which he needs absolutely for his formation, just
> as he needs food to build up his body.[8]

A realistic view of the human condition, no doubt, but does it really account for the universality of sin?

Other authors take a similar situational view of original sin.[9] Louis Monden argues that a child, before he can consciously experience his freedom, is profoundly influenced by "all the greed, the cupidity, the pride, the divisions, quarrels and jealousies" of the human community.[10] For Monden, original sin is a situation

> brought about in mankind from the very beginning,
> an initial option which keeps spreading more widely
> as mankind expands and growing stronger with the
> individual sins of each person. On the other hand,
> each man, even before he is able to use his freedom,
> is by the very fact of being historically situated within
> mankind, unavoidably caught up in the sphere of
> influence of that evil, as an area of darkness which
> he cannot conquer by his own power and which holds
> him back from the meeting with God.[11]

According to Sharon MacIsaac, the doctrine of original sin conveys the truth that man "is formed by his environment at a level anterior to choice,"[12] and she asks whether such an explanation of sin in terms of environmental influences can adequately convey the meaning of the traditional formula *propagatione non imitatione*. She answers in the affirmative:

> It can, surely, if environmental influences are under-
> stood not in the superficial Pelagian sense of examples
> that are freely chosen for imitation, but in the pro-
> found sense brought into fresh prominence by the
> investigation of Freud and the social sciences. In this
> sense, the child is born into a situation which is sinful
> (as well as wholesome), and one which forms him
> before he can choose with respect to it. It is operative
> from the moment of birth.[13]

Christian Duquoc describes the "sin of the world" as "the tangle of responsibilities and errors which constitute human reality in its reciprocal interdependence as deaf to the appeal from God."[14] Duquoc identifies this tendency to interpret original sin as the "sin of the world" along with a shift in emphasis from "historical ante-cedence" to "eschatological dynamism" as the two main lines of approach in the current reinterpretation of the Catholic doctrine of original sin. The latter tendency involves a more processive, evo-lutionary view which sees original sin not so much as the unhappy residue of some past event but as "the opposition at present between our history and the dynamism of the ultimate'';[15] that is, as the contradiction between what we are and what we are called to become in Christ.

The theology of the sin of the world raises at least two questions. In the first place, when original sin is identified as the sin of the world does it really provide an adequate reinterpretation of the word *generation*? In trying to expand the meaning of *generation* so as to avoid the unacceptable association of sin with the procreative act, have we ended by branding as sinful the whole process of nurturing and educating our children? Moreover, the expanded understanding of *generation* in the authors quoted above sounds suspiciously more like imitation than generation; unless, of course, one restricts the meaning of imitation to conscious, freely chosen imitation. This may indeed be true to the intent of the Tridentine formula to condemn a Pelagian view of original sin. But could one not argue also that another obvious intent of the formula was to identify, in the terms it had available to it, original sin as a given of individual human nature rather than something contracted from the environment?[16]

Secondly, perhaps the two lines of reinterpretation mentioned above (the situational and the evolutionary) are not entirely compatible. Does not the concept of the sin of the world, inviting as it does the vision of an increasingly sinful situation in which the human person must live, come into conflict with the more optimistic vision of eschatological fulfillment as the culmination of the historical process of human striving? If the individual sees himself as hopelessly enmeshed in a sinful world, his options would appear to be either to turn away from the world and seek a very individualistic type of salvation; or to pursue a path of idealism in which his own self-authentication and the salvation of the world become matters of human achievement—an attitude which is the antithesis of faith. I want to suggest that the ''consciousness of sin'' which is the necessary precondition of faith comes, not so much from the realization of one's solidarity with sinful humanity, but from the realization of the inadequacy of one's own and human civilization's ''good works'' to authenticate or justify one's existence. For St. Paul, faith becomes possible only when one is convinced of the inadequacy of the ''works of the law.''

The view, therefore, that our need for redemption becomes convincingly apparent only at the point of our highest religious, moral, and cultural achievements seems to me to fit best with the evolutionary view of original sin mentioned above. Only such a view finds a place for human progress and initiative (as the necessary preamble to faith), for salvation is then seen not merely as the rescue of individuals from a hopelessly sinful world, but as the eschatological achieving of the transcendent goal of human striving; namely, the goal which is beyond human achievement. It is this ambiguity of all human achievement which Theodore Roszak describes as the "terrible paradox of progress which gives us this world where things get worse as they get better."[17] According to Karl Barth, making us aware of this paradox is the function of "religion." For the more we achieve in the way of religious observance, the more we are convinced of the inadequacy of that observance to form a justifying relationship with God:

> Religion compels us to the conception that God is not
> to be found in religion. Religion makes us to know
> that we are competent to advance no single step. Reli-
> gion, as the final human possibility, commands us to
> halt. Religion brings us to the place where we must
> wait, in order that God may confront us—on the other
> side of the frontier of religion.[18]

In this view the formula which best describes the human condition would not be "the more sinful man becomes the more he realizes his need for redemption," but rather "the more religious he becomes the more he realizes his need for redemption"; or, in Roszak's words, "things get worse as they get better." The "sin of the world" concept, on the other hand, seems to give us a vision of the world in which "things get worse," without reminding us of the paradoxical truth that this happens precisely "as they get better."

It is at this point, I believe, that a psychoanalytic interpretation of the word *generation* might prove helpful to the discussion. Whereas the "sin of the world" concept accounts for the inevitability and universality of sin in terms of the injurious environmental influences brought to bear on the child before he is capable of conscious moral choices, the psychoanalytic view of human growth locates the origins of guilt precisely in the attempts of those in the child's environment to transmit moral values. Applying this insight to the doctrine of original sin involves reinterpreting the word *genera-tion* in the light of a concept such as Erik Erikson's "generativity." For Erikson, this term represents a logical extension of Freud's psychosexual model of human development. For Freud, the cul-mination of that development was the achieving of genital sexuality in young adulthood. Erikson expands this view of human becoming by pointing out that sexual intimacy "leads to a gradual expansion of ego interests and to a libidinal investment in that which is being generated."[19] This "libidinal investment" is what Erikson calls generativity, which he defines as "the concern in establishing and guiding the next generation."[20]

Like the concept of the sin of the world, the concept of gener-ativity calls for an interpretation of the word *generation*, not as the isolated procreative act but as a process. In this case, however, the process is no longer the negative one of being gradually assimilated into a sinful environment with the resulting evil consequences, but rather the process of parenting, nurturing, and educating in which humanity does, not its worst to corrupt the child, but its best to transmit moral principles and values. But in keeping with our pre-viously stated paradoxical view of the human condition, psycho-analytic theory suggests that it is precisely in the process of inter-nalizing such moral principles that the child first experiences guilt or, in religious language, the consciousness of sin.

To understand this paradox, it is helpful to recall the follow-ing features of Freudian theory which we have already discussed. (1) Freud maintains that the most fundamental conflict in human existence is the conflict between the unifying life instinct (Eros) and the destructive and divisive death instinct. (2) Civilization is a "pro-cess in the service of Eros" since by sublimating sexuality and repressing aggressiveness (an externalized expression of the death instinct) it tries to create the conditions necessary for the triumph of Eros over death. (3) This process of civilization turns out to be self-defeating since, under the influence of civilization's repressions, aggression is once again internalized and is experienced in the form of guilt since the energy of the repressed aggressiveness is appro-priated by the superego and turned against one's own ego. The death instinct is now experienced in the form of guilt. (4) The inter-nalizing of cultural prohibitions takes place, in the first instance, during the Oedipal phase of the child's development. As the child grows, the same internalizing of authority will take place in wider forms of communal life beyond the family. Thus the "loss of happiness through heightening the sense of guilt," which Freud saw as the price of such internalizing of authority, is continually reinforced.

Notice that while Freud agrees the child arrives at a sense of guilt through contact with his environment, the nature of the contact is entirely different from that suggested by the theology of the sin of the world. In Freud's view, it is not culture's evil influences which foster the sense of guilt in the individual. Rather it is culture's best efforts on the individual's behalf: the effort of his parents to transmit cultural and moral values, and the effort of cultural institutions to lead mankind to the goal of civilization's "erotic impulsion," that is, to the ultimate "unity of mankind" (the kingdom of God?). These efforts inevitably produce the sense of guilt.

Why must this be so? Why must civilized man's noblest efforts be self-defeating? Freud's answer is that the root of the problem is not in mankind's cultural institutions but in individual human nature, in the instinctual duality of Eros and death. For Freud, the negative destructive impulses exist apart from civilization, just as for St. Paul sin exists apart from the law. "Sin was in the world before the law was given, but sin is not counted where there is no law" (Rom. 5:13). Sin, as a given of human existence, becomes painfully apparent through the transgressions of the law which it inspires. Guilt, therefore, as the painful awareness of sin, is the result of man's encounter with the law. This is in agreement with the Freudian view that guilt is the result of man's encounter with civilization's cultural repressions. Both Freud and St. Paul seem to agree that sin, conceived of as a divisive and alienating egoism which opposes that "life" which is the object of both civilized and religious man's striving, is rooted in the individual human nature, and what is produced by man's contact with his cultural and religious environment is not sin, but the consciousness of it, namely, guilt.

What then is transmitted by "generation"? If by generation we mean the whole process of parenting, nurturing, and educating suggested by Erikson's "generativity," then what is transmitted is a sense of guilt. Now guilt implies personal responsibility, and it is in the transgressions of religious and cultural prohibitions that this responsibility is felt. But at the same time it is recognized that there is an involuntary aspect to the "sin" which inspires such transgressions. This involuntary aspect—this "law in my members" —is an existential given and, therefore, the universal condition of humankind. In any doctrine of original sin there is a tension between these two elements, universality and personal responsibility. The obvious intent of the Adamic myth is to explain the universality of sin. It could be noted here, in passing, that the Freudian theory of the primal horde may be read as a similar type of myth. For Christianity, all men repeat the sin of Adam; for Freud, all men, in the Oedipal experience, relive the guilt-producing experience of the primal horde.

In both cases, however, the myth gives expression to a truth of human existence without explaining it in terms of historical causality. If we adopt the eschatological view of original sin mentioned above, then sin becomes the universal condition of unredeemed humanity, or the contradiction between our present existence and our essential being that can only be realized in the eschatological fulfillment promised in Christ. This painful experience of the gap between actual existence and essential being is the universal experience of humankind, and it represents the involuntary aspect of sin.

Perhaps it is therefore necessary to retain both meanings of the term *generation*, as referring both to the event of conception and birth and to the generative process described by Erikson. To be born is to enter into human existence and to assume, therefore, this alienation from one's essential being which is the mark of that existence. Generation, then, may be taken in the first instance to refer to the entry of each individual into human existence, which for Paul Tillich represents a "fall" from essence to existence, an entry into the finite of one who belongs to the infinite.[21] But generation can also be understood as that process by which each individual becomes aware of his real condition; that is, the religious and cultural process of "eating of the tree of the knowledge of good and evil," of internalizing moral and cultural values. This process, as we have seen, carries with it the sense of guilt and personal responsibility. Both these interpretations of the term *generation* are in fundamental disagreement with that proposed by the theology of the "sin of the world." Generation as "birth" suggests a personalist, rather than a situational, understanding of original sin. Sin is seen as a given of individual human nature rather than something assimilated from the environment. Generation as a process, on the other hand, is seen as a fundamentally different kind of process from that suggested by the concept of the sin of the world. Sin is not the result of harmful environmental influences; sin, or rather our awareness of it, is paradoxically the result of beneficial environmental influences. The Freudian contention that our guilt and discontent, and hence our domination by the death instinct, are the result of our internalizing of moral and cultural values is in keeping with the biblical imagery which depicts Adam and Eve expelled from paradise and the "tree of life" as the result of their eating of the "tree of the knowledge of good and evil."

Redemption

I have suggested that the ultimate human and religious question is "Can life prevail against death?" and that this question provides the most fruitful point of intersection for dialogue between Freudian psychoanalysis and Christian theology. Thus far we have noted two fundamental points of agreement between Christian and Freudian thought in dealing with this question. (1) Both deal with the problem of human existence in the fundamental categories of life and death, and, as we have seen, "life" in each case is conceived of as an interpersonal and communal reality. (2) Both Christian and Freudian thought are pessimistic about the capacity of human nature and human civilization to bring about a triumph of life over death. Christianity's hope and optimism are based on belief in a transcendent source of life and therefore the possibility of redemption from death in the form of guilt. The triumph of life over death becomes possible through the experience of redemption and salvation.

In order to more fully compare the Freudian and Christian responses to the question of life and death, it is necessary to examine the meaning of redemption and salvation as an experience in which life triumphs over death. It must be made clear, however, that we are not speaking of salvation in terms of an afterlife but as an experience of one's present existence, for it is only in this sense that salvation can be accessible to psychological analysis or interpreted within the context of a psychological understanding of the human condition. What we are concerned with, then, in our present context, is an analysis of that experience of personal transformation and self-transcendence which is conveyed by the words *grace* and *faith*. I believe that it is precisely in his analysis of this experience that St. Paul answers the question "Can life prevail over death?" To compare his answer with that of Freud is not to suggest that they answer the question in the same way, but to suggest: (1) that the Freudian analysis of the human condition in terms of the struggle between Eros and the death instinct may help to clarify the Christian understanding of life and death (understood as qualities of one's present existence); and (2) that, to the extent Eros approximates the Christian understanding of "life," faith may be understood as what makes possible the victory of Eros over death, and therefore Paul's analysis of the role of faith as the precondition of "life" may be read as his "answer to Freud."

In chapters 5, 6, and 7 of Romans, Paul analyzes the human condition by dividing human history into three stages which represent three possible existential conditions: living without law, under the law, and under grace (and therefore liberated from the law). Faith for Paul was the radical act of trust by which the believer transcended the moral, religious, and psychological conflicts occasioned by his attempts to observe the Mosaic law. But the ensuing description of the dynamics of faith is prototypical since the Mosaic law represents only one means of self-justification. There are other types of "law" by which, in my attempts to obey, I discover another frustrating law "in my members." The Mosaic law, therefore, becomes a prototype for all human efforts to live a self-justifying or self-authenticating existence through reliance on one's own human resources.

This attempt at self-justification through legal, religious, and moral observance leads to a psychological state which Paul does not hesitate to describe as "death," and it is only by transcending the law through the act and commitment of faith that one is "delivered from this body of death." Paul's three stages of human history, therefore, refer also to the three stages of the development of faith, or the three psychological states through which one passes in arriving at faith. The believer, living under grace, sees himself in retrospect as having reached that level of existence by first passing through those psychological states that correspond to Paul's historical periods from Adam to Moses (without law) and from Moses to Christ (under the law).

1. Living without Law   For Paul this stage refers historically to the period from Adam to Moses (i.e., the period preceding the giving of the law through Moses), and psychologically to the period of childhood before the development of conscience and moral values. It was only with the giving of the law through Moses that humankind became more conscious of its guilt, just as it is only through commitment to moral and ethical values that the individual becomes painfully aware of his lack of moral rectitude. In terms of life and death, this stage is one of illusion and ignorance—a stage in which we enjoy the illusion of life because we are ignorant of our real situation in the absence of any law to make us aware of the existence of sin within us. "Sin indeed was in the world before the law was given, but sin is not counted where there is no law" (Rom. 5:13).

The result of such ignorance is the illusion that one is "alive." For Paul, sin came into the world with Adam and was therefore operative in the world from that time, but the individual is not conscious of his sin and guilt except through his transgressions of the law. When this happens the illusion of "life" gives way to the experience of "death." "I was once alive apart from the law, but when the commandment came sin revived and I died; the very commandment which promised life proved to be death" (Rom. 7:9-10).

2. Living under the Law   With the giving of the law comes the painful awareness of guilt, inadequacy, and incompleteness. The law was good in itself, but it brings with it the awareness of one's basic sinfulness through one's transgressions of the law. "What then shall we say? That the law is sin? By no means! Yet, if it had not been for the law, I should not have known sin. I should not have known what it is to covet if the law had not said, 'You shall not covet' " (Rom. 7:7).

The ultimate effect of the law is to produce anxiety because the individual's failure to observe it makes him aware of the existential gap between himself as he knows he should be and himself as he actually exists when he grounds his existence in his own human resources. In other words, the individual's anxiety results from the dichotomy he experiences between his knowledge and his will. He knows the good to be done through his knowledge of the law, but his will is often powerless to act on this knowledge. Paul describes the conflict graphically:

> We know that the law is spiritual; but I am carnal,
> sold under sin. I do not understand my own actions.
> For I do not do what I want but I do the very thing

I hate. Now if I do what I do not want, I agree that the law is good. So then it is no longer I that do it, but sin which dwells within me. For I know that nothing good dwells within me, that is, in my flesh. I can will what is right, but I cannot do it. For I do not do the good I want, but the evil I do not want is what I do. Now if I do what I do not want, it is no longer I that do it, but sin which dwells within me. (Rom. 7:14-20)

In his commentary on this passage, Joseph Fitzmeyer describes the conflict experienced by Paul—and by every person who seeks justification through observance of a "law"—as "the cleavage between his reason-dominated desire and his actual performance,"[22] and this awareness or consciousness of sin is occasioned by the law, which, by creating awareness of transgression, makes one aware of the basic condition of sin that lies behind every individual transgression. In itself the law is just and good (Rom. 7:12) and therefore is not the direct cause of sin, and thus death. The ultimate source of death is that basic condition of sin which Stanislas Lyonnet, in a passage quoted above, describes as "that deeply rooted egoism by which man, since original sin, orientates everything to himself instead of opening himself to God and to others."[23] If, therefore, Paul describes the law as the occasion of his "death," he is clearly using the word *death* to describe the experience of guilt, anxiety, and inner conflict which resulted from the painful awareness of his "deeply rooted egoism," an awareness brought about, in turn, by his attempts to keep the law. As we have seen, Freud had his own explanation of why that experience of guilt should be labelled "death."

3. Living under Grace The law causes anxiety and guilt ("death") only as long as an individual feels that he must justify himself before God by keeping the law. But faith delivers him from this anxiety because in faith he believes that the justifying relationship with God he is seeking is not something earned through moral and religious observance but a free and unmerited gift of God (grace). Thus relieved of the necessity of justifying himself through moralistic striving, the believer enters into a personal relationship with God that transcends the merely ethical or legal relationship of "man under the law." For the believer, this means that the transformation he tries unsuccessfully to bring about through moralistic striving and legal observance is ultimately achieved only through God's act of forgiveness and acceptance in Christ. Believing that he is accepted by God in spite of his guilt and is forgiven, he is liberated from the necessity of self-justification and is free to serve God and his neighbour out of the love and gratitude resulting from a personal relationship.

This dynamic of the faith experience has its analogue in the process of human development. The pre-Oedipal stage of childhood represents a state of being "without law." The child at this stage is extroverted and "outer-directed"; he is busy discovering the external world. "Sin" exists in the form of negative, destructive impulses and behaviour—in the form of egoism—but the experience of guilt and anxiety does not begin until the internalizing of moral values and codes of behaviour begins at the Oedipal stage. In the meantime he experiences only the fear of punishment—not the need for punishment. Developmentally, the stage of being "under the law" begins at the Oedipal stage and continues through adolescence. During this time a gradual process of becoming more introspective and "inner-directed" takes place. The values and ideals of the child's family and culture become, to some extent, his own. They become "the law" in the sense in which Paul used the word; that is, they become norms of conduct which serve as a means of "justifying" oneself—proving oneself worthy and acceptable. Hence the well-known idealism and self-consciousness of adolescence. But such preoccupation with oneself—with one's worthiness and acceptability—must be outgrown if one is to become an adult and assume adult responsibilities; for it is the hallmark of adulthood to "become a child again"; that is, to become outer-directed again and to be concerned not with oneself but with the responsibilities of occupational, marital, and social life. To make this transition, the adolescent must have an experience analogous to the experience of grace—an experience of unconditional acceptance by the significant others in his life—which relieves him of the burden of constantly proving himself and earning the acceptance of others. Only in this way can he transcend his preoccupation with himself. At both the human and the religious level the same truth obtains: only through the experience of grace, of unconditional acceptance, does one achieve self-transcendence, and, therefore, human and religious maturity.

As far as it can be analyzed psychologically, this transformation effected by faith could be described as—to use Gordon Allport's phrase—a "transformation of motives." According to Paul, the believer overcomes the "death" occasioned by the law because by grace he is liberated from the law itself and is permitted to live "the new life of the Spirit" (Rom. 6:6). What the believer is liberated from, however, is the "oppression" of the law, that is, the necessity of justifying himself by observing and fulfilling the law. Thus the believer is liberated from the law, not objectively (through some kind of abrogation of law), for the law is still objectively valid and expresses valid moral principles to which the believer is committed (Rom. 7:12, 22), but subjectively, in that he acquires a new attitude to the law and a new motive for observing it. This new attitude and motive are based on the premise that God's acceptance is unconditional; it is not conditional upon one's ability to keep the law. Hence the possibility is created of moral and religious observance—including the love of one's neighbour—based on self-transcending rather than self-justifying motives.

Karl Barth speaks of the transformation of motives as permitting one's love to be what it should be, occupied with the object of one's love and not with one's own needs:

> It amounts to this, that in love man is occupied with
> something else, and he ought always to be so. It would
> completely destroy the essential character of Christian
> love as the freedom given to man and to be kept by
> man if we tried to burden it with the, in itself, impos-
> sible and superfluous task of accomplishing or actual-
> izing or even completing the justification of man.[24]

The relationship between faith and love, from a psychological point of view, seems to consist precisely in this: that the love of the believer for God and his fellow human beings is free, spontaneous, and altruistic ("functionally autonomous," to use Allport's phrase) to the extent that his life is built on faith. The love of the person of faith is given freely because he has received freely (Matt. 10:8); it is concerned with its object rather than with self-justification because in the light of grace, self-justification has become futile. This spontaneous, self-transcending love, which the New Testament calls agape, is the vital principle of the life of faith that overcomes the "death" occasioned by the law and makes possible that unity which is the aim of Freud's life instinct (Eros).

For Paul, two things conspire to bring about an individual's "death": the sin that dwells in him and the law which makes him painfully aware of it. For Freud, likewise, the cause of death is two-fold: the biologically rooted death instinct and man's encounter with the repressions of civilization, which, like the law, produce guilt and make possible the death instinct's domination of the opposing life instinct (Eros).

In Freud's view, however, the cure for the civilized person's discontent and unhappiness does not consist in the removal of civilization's repressions to allow a return to the "natural" state, just as Paul did not propose the abolition of law as a cure for the anxiety and frustration experienced "under the law." In this context, Freud's assessment of natural man as opposed to civilized man is analogous to that existential state described by Paul as living without the law; in both instances, what is described is a state of illusion and ignorance. For Paul, this natural state is the state which precedes our guilt-producing encounter with the law; it is a state in which sin prevails though one is not fully conscious of it, and therefore has the illusion of being "alive," whereas in fact "death reigns." This analysis is based on the premise that sin, in the form of the basic condition of egoism, is within the individual—a part of the human condition—and not the result of the law, which, as we have seen, is merely the occasion for awareness of one's sinful condition.

In the same way, Freud locates the source of repression in the dualism of human nature itself rather than in the religious, social, and cultural institutions of civilization which man creates as a means of carrying out the necessary repression on himself. The negative, destructive impulses exist apart from civilization just as sin exists apart from the law. Apart from civilization, he insists, we live at the mercy of these destructive impulses. If the attempt were not made to create civilization, then human relationships "would be subject to the arbitrary will of the individual: that is to say, the physically stronger man would decide them in the sense of his own interests and instinctual impulses."[25] Paul wants to dispel our illusions about the "life" enjoyed before the encounter with the law; in the same way, Freud wants to dispel our illusions about the natural goodness of man apart from civilization's repressions, especially that illusion's most popular form—the innocence of child-hood. For both Freud and Paul, childhood is the stage of illusion and ignorance—a state of sin (sexual and aggressive strivings) without guilt. The illusion is shattered for Paul by the guilt-producing encounter with the law; for Freud, by the guilt-producing encounter with civilization and its repressions.

Thus the function of civilization is analogous to that of the law for Paul: both represent extraneous authorities that promise life but deliver death in the form of guilt.

And now perhaps we are in a position to clarify the meaning of that "death" which Paul experienced as the result of his frustrating attempts to justify himself through observance of the law; for Paul's (and everyone's) encounter with the law served only to reinforce that sense of guilt which Freud identifies as a manifestation of the death instinct. The plight of Paul's man under the law is but one instance of the plight of civilized man in general; both had sought life and found death.

Unlike Paul, who finds a way of transcending this "body of death" through faith and grace, Freud can only base his hope for some kind of victory of Eros over death in the possibility of mankind's discovering some form of civilization which represents an "expedient accommodation—one that will bring happiness—between this claim of the individual and the cultural claims of the group."[26] In other words, while Paul looks for life in the transcending of and liberation from the law, Freud looks for a law (civilization) that can give life. I have suggested that Paul's analysis of the role of faith as a precondition of "life" can be read as an "answer to Freud," but this is true only if the life which Paul sees as issuing from faith and grace means the same to Paul as Eros does to Freud. In what way is the "life" experienced by the believer similar to the Eros described by Freud? However, since the essence of "life" in the Christian sense is, as we have seen, that spontaneous love which concerns itself with its object and is free of self-preoccupation—the New Testament agape—our question has to do with the relationship of the Freudian Eros to the Christian agape.

In his classic work *Agape and Eros*, Anders Nygren attempted to clarify the meaning of agape and to distinguish it from the Platonic eros. In *Life against Death* Norman O. Brown suggests that the Freudian concept of Eros transcends both the "aggressiveness" of the Platonic eros and the "masochism" of the Christian agape.

I want to suggest rather that the Freudian concept of Eros is closer to the authentic meaning of agape than it is to the Platonic eros; that, in fact, it helps to restore the authentic meaning of agape. If this be the case, then the faith that makes agape possible may be interpreted psychoanalytically as that which makes possible the triumph of Eros over death. The Christian agape and the Freudian Eros resemble each other in at least two respects: they are both described as objective unifying forces and as being beyond the realm of human achievement.

We have seen that the Christian ideal of love is attained only through the self-transcending quality of faith, in view of which the believer, relieved of the necessity of self-justification, is enabled to love spontaneously—with what Nygren called an "unmotivated love." Agape is not the result of human obedience to the commandment of love, but the result of a genuine transformation of motives which takes place as the result of one's faith response to God's agape. Agape is not merely a law to be obeyed, but a power released in the human subject through the transforming effect of faith and grace. Paul describes the vital principle of this transformation, of this new life and new relationship with God, as the spirit of God who gives the believer an inner capacity to love which the law could not give. The love that is the essence of this new life is not a human achievement, but the love of God which "has been poured into our hearts through the Holy Spirit which has been given to us" (Rom. 5:5). Nygren states:

> This divine Agape infused by the Holy Spirit forms
> the real substance of the Christian life, and in the life
> that Christians lead among their fellow men it is meant
> to be passed on to others. The Christian has nothing
> of his own to give; the love which he shows to his
> neighbour is the love which God has infused into
> him.[27]

If, therefore, the term agape can be used to describe not only God's freely given love but also human love for one's neighbour, it is not because of any human capability of achieving the same kind of unmotivated altruistic love as God but because the love of God is present as an objective force in the form of God's Spirit and is operative in the human community. In order to make agape a human achievement it must be turned into an observable law, a process that completely destroys the character of agape by turning it into a dutiful kind of love for those whom we cannot love spontaneously (loving those we cannot "like"). When Joseph Fletcher, in his *Situation Ethics: The New Morality*, described agape as the love of benevolence—the only kind of love that could be commanded—he completely reversed the meaning of agape, which is precisely the kind of love that cannot be commanded since it is God's love and not a human achievement. Agape is not a legal and moral ideal which one can achieve through willpower, but a power released through the presence of God's agape. It is for this reason that Christian morality cannot be reduced to one absolute— the law of love—for law "kills" us by occasioning that guilt which Freud saw as deriving from the death instinct, and faith involves the transcending of law as such, even the law of love. Agape, as the New Testament sees it, is the result of an objective force (the Spirit) operative in the human community creating a love and unity in which "there is neither Jew nor Greek, there is neither slave nor free, there is neither male nor female" (Gal. 3:28) and which we cannot achieve through our own unaided moral striving.

The same characteristics, I believe, are observable in Freud's description of Eros—the life instinct. Eros is an objective force bringing about a unity that is beyond human achievement. Freud saw human personality as resulting from the objective causality of physiological drives such as Eros and the death instinct, and he emphasized the primacy of such drives. The neo-Freudian and humanistic reactions to Freud were a rejection, not simply of the primacy of the sex instincts in human personality, but of the primacy of the physiological drives as such, in favour of a more "subjective" psychology which makes personality the creation of the individual ego in pursuit of self-defined goals. In Freudian theory the ego does not establish its own goals in any ultimate sense; it directs the energy of the instincts towards those objectives in the environment which will gratify their aims.

This instinctual aim is usually described as homeostasis—a tensionless state which is consistent with the aim of the death instinct. Freud could say at one point in the development of his theory that "the aim of life is death," but, as we have seen, in his final *Outline of Psychoanalysis*,[28] Eros becomes the exception to this general rule of instinctual life because it is the antithesis of death,

which it resists. Paul Ricoeur describes Eros and death as two different forces which may dominate either the sex or ego instincts.[29]
Indeed, they are forces operative at every level of life, biological,
psychological, and social. Eros, therefore, is not merely identical
with human sexual or erotic impulses but represents an objective
force present at the heart not only of human existence but of nature
itself, impelling it towards the goal of unity. It is in this respect
that it approaches the meaning of agape. It is the striving for this
goal of unity which Freud saw as the struggle for life—the triumph
of Eros—and the motive force behind the development of
civilization.

In describing Eros, the life instinct, which Freud also referred to as the
"love instinct,"[30] appears as an objective force impelling all of
nature towards the goal of unity. In a similar vein, Paul speaks
of the love of God—agape—as being present among us as an objective force (the Spirit) and impelling us towards the same goal of
unity. This does not mean, of course, that the unity created by
what Paul identifies as the Spirit of God can be reduced to the
Freudian life instinct. It does suggest, however, that whatever the
merits of Freud's theory of instincts, it lends support to the idea
that what Paul sees as the unifying activity of the Spirit is correlative
with our deepest human aspirations.

In describing civilization as a "process in the service of
Eros," Freud recognized both these aspirations towards love and
unity and the impossibility of their fulfillment. Civilization is created
in order to ensure the triumph of Eros over death. Freud recognized
that the goal of unity could not be achieved through practical con-
siderations, such as the advantages of community life, but only
through the establishing of "libidinal ties" of friendship and affection among people. Hence the sublimation of sexuality towards
"aim-inhibited" goals. At the same time, he was aware that civilization ultimately fails in its efforts to make Eros prevail over death
because its weapon is guilt, which results from the repression of
aggressiveness, thereby giving expression to the death instinct and
weakening Eros.

Freud's analysis of the human dilemma amounts to this:
while we desire life, our attempt to make life prevail against death
ultimately ends in failure, frustration, and discontent. Eros is just
as clearly beyond the realm of human achievement as is agape.
Paul's "answer to Freud" is that there is no law (civilization) that

can give life, for that love which is the vital principle of the life we seek is beyond human achievement. Only the gift of God's agape, received in faith, makes Eros possible.

The Meaning of Culture

Theological reflection on the meaning of "salvation" has revolved, in part at least, around the tension of the personal versus the social, and even cosmic, meanings of the word. Is salvation to be understood as the transcendent goal of the historical-cultural process or as the transcendent goal of individual human becoming? If salvation refers to an eschatological event and fulfillment, is it to be interpreted in terms of an eschatology which is "vertical" and existential or one that is "horizontal" and historical? Is salvation to be understood as personal transformation or as transformation of the social order? Does the phrase "kingdom of God" refer, as in liberation theology, to the transcendent goal of the historical process by which the human community struggles to liberate itself from social, economic, and political oppression? Or are we to see the kingdom of God as essentially "within," resisting all attempts to externalize and objectify what is essentially a symbol for the inner psychic reality of human striving for greater wholeness and integration? Does the "new creation" refer to social revolution or individual rebirth?

Our discussion of Freud and St. Paul has focused on the experience of redemption and salvation as one of personal transformation. As far as it can be described psychologically this transformation was seen to be a transformation of motives—a self-transcending experience brought about through the experience of grace and faith and making possible to some degree a kind of self-transcending love (agape) which is consistent with the goal of Eros. In that discussion the following points of comparison emerged. (1) Both Freud and St. Paul are concerned with the same fundamental and essentially religious question: Can life triumph over death? (2) Both are capable only of a pessimistic answer to this question on the basis of their respective analyses of the human condition. For Paul, outside of the experience of grace and faith one remains "under the law," and all attempts to authenticate one's existence through observance of the law only result in the experience of death in the form of guilt. It is that same sense of guilt which Freud identified as both the derivative and the manifestation of the death instinct and which is the inevitable fate of civilized man. As we have seen, the plight of Paul's man under the law is but one instance of the plight of civilized man in general; both had sought life and found death. (3) Both St. Paul and Freud pronounce an apparently negative judgement on the law and civilization respectively since these are ultimately self-defeating and end in the experience of death (guilt). But this negative judgement is only apparent since the law (civilization) is seen as merely the *occasion* for the experience of death. Ultimately the source of death is within individual human nature: for Freud, in the biologically rooted death instinct; and for Paul, in the sin which dwells within the individual and of which he becomes aware only through the law.

Given these similarities, can theology judge civilization (culture) in the same way that St. Paul judges the law; that is, as the occasion and context for that experience of "death" which is the necessary precondition for the experience of faith and life? In other words, can we make use of the Freudian theory of culture to construct a theology of culture and to interpret the meaning of salvation in the social-historical meaning of the word? We have seen that both culture and the law frustrate the human pursuit of life and lead in fact to the experience of death (guilt). Moreover, we have also seen that the life which becomes possible for St. Paul through the freedom from the law which comes with the experience of grace and faith, and which has as its vital principle that self-transcending love the New Testament calls agape, is, like the Freudian Eros, essentially *interpersonal*. Agape is—to use Nygren's phrase— "unmotivated love"; namely, love which transcends the self-justifying striving of one who is "under the law" and creates an interpersonal unity with the other which is free of such self-preoccupation, and which is consistent with that unity of living substances which is the aim of Eros.

If, therefore, human salvation means the attaining of "life" in this sense of the word, would a theology of culture involve an evaluation of culture which assigns to it the same kind of propae-deutic role which Paul assigns to the law? In this case, culture would be viewed, like the individual's moral striving under the law, as an area of human achievement whose limitations we must experience as a necessary precondition for the experience of life. Such a theological interpretation of culture involves a transposing of Paul's existential experience onto the social, cultural, and historical plane. In the Christian perspective one must die in order to live. For Paul this meant that the death (guilt) induced by the law is a precondition of life. On the cultural and historical level it would mean that the ultimate triumph of life over death cannot be achieved apart from the death- (guilt-) producing process of civilization. That process becomes the larger context for that painful experience of one's finitude, guilt, and need for redemption which Paul experienced at the dead end of his attempts to observe the law. I have already suggested that the Freudian view of culture suggests the notion of transcendence in the sense described by Tillich as the tendency of the finite to "point beyond itself" for, like Paul's encounter with the law, the process of civilization and the ambiguity of all cultural achievements bring us to that "boundary situation" in which faith becomes possible.

I want to suggest that this transposition of Paul's existential experience "under the law" to the cultural and historical plane is precisely what has happened in the shift in theological reflection from theological existentialism and salvation as personal transformation to the more future-oriented theologies of hope and liberation, which, as we saw in our discussion of natural theology, interpret eschatology as horizontal and historical, and salvation as the transcendent goal of the historical process. If we define eschatology as that question in theology which deals with the object of Christian hope—the kingdom of God, the new creation—then the theologies of hope and liberation represent the most recent development in the understanding of this question. The development of the doctrine of eschatology began with the future expectations of the early Christians, who looked for the literal destruction of their physical world and the creation of a new world. In the course of time the end of the world came to be understood as the departure of the individual from this life and this world. Thus, the eschatological questions were the questions of death, judgement, heaven, and hell, as an examination of the old theology manuals reminds us. In this understanding eschatology referred to a personal transformation, but in terms of an afterlife. It was the theological existentialists who gave a much needed emphasis to the fact that this transformation begins within our present existence. The eschatological moment is now seen as the moment of personal transformation through the experience of grace and faith, that is, the "vertical" action of God upon the individual which results in what Rudolph Bultmann called "a new understanding'' of one's existence. In the theologies of hope and liberation, eschatology is understood as historical and cultural. While not denying the necessity of personal transformation, these theologies focus on an eschatological transformation of the world. The eschatological goal is not only the transcendent goal of human growth but the transcendent goal of the ''horizontal'' process of culture and history.

Though both these emphases—the personal and the social/historical—are essential to a complete understanding of eschatological fulfillment, the shift in focus does permit an extension of Paul's understanding of ''law'' to include the historical process of civilization. That process now becomes another instance of ''law,'' namely, a realm of human achievement which promises life but delivers death. In this new theological perspective in which salvation is interpreted in terms of humanity's hope for the future and desire for liberation, guilt and the need for redemption are experienced not only through the inadequacies of the individual's moral striving ''under the law,'' but also through the inadequacy of civilization's cultural and historical achievements. This process represents humanity's attempt at self-justification or self-authentication—the human attempt to transform not just the individual but the world of human society. It is in this process that we observe—to recall Theodore Roszak's words—that ''things get worse as they get better.'' Hence a theology of culture which, like Freud's theory of culture, emphasizes the essential ambiguity of all cultural achievements.

This extension of Paul's understanding of the law begins within theological existentialism itself. For Paul, what the believer transcends in the faith experience is his guilt-producing attempts at self-justification through observance of the Mosaic law. But, as we have seen, the Mosaic law represents only one means of self-justification, so that, in a more general way, faith may be described as the act by which one transcends all guilt-producing efforts to live a self-justifying or self-authenticating existence through one's own human resources.

It is interesting to observe how this notion of ''the law'' is elaborated by those theological existentialists who analyze the same experience of grace and faith and to whom we have made reference in our discussion of natural theology. What, for Paul, is a transition from law to grace is for Sören Kierkegaard a ''leap'' from the ethical to the religious level of existence; for Rudolf Bultmann it is a transition from the frustrating knowledge of authentic human existence arrived at through philosophical speculation which leaves one powerless to realize that existence, to the transforming realization of authentic existence made possible by faith; and for Paul Tillich it is a liberation from all estrangement-producing attempts to find the "courage to be" in something finite (oneself or one's world) and the discovery of that courage in the infinite ground of one's being. In this extended meaning "law" refers to all those self-imposed burdens by which one attempts to justify one's existence. These include all forms of moralistic striving which represent the self-consciously religious person's attempts at self-justification (Kierkegaard's ethical life) as well as all forms of self-actualization by which the individual—religious or non-religious—attempts to authenticate his existence, such as philosophical insight (Bultmann) or strivings towards autonomy or self-affirmation (Tillich).

In transposing this dynamic to the cultural and historical plane, the process of civilization itself becomes the self-imposed burden by which humanity tries to achieve authentic human existence. This is consistent with the Freudian view that civilization is created in order to carry out those repressions which will allow Eros to triumph over death. In the theologies of hope and liberation God becomes the power of the future which transcends the limitations of the present; that is, the limitations of civilization and its repressions, which are painfully experienced as death in the form of guilt. It is interesting to note in this regard that just as Paul finds the ultimate source of the human experience of "death," not in the law, but in that sin or egoism which is part and parcel of human nature, in the same way the theology of liberation does not ultimately account for human oppression merely in terms of oppressive social and economic structures but looks also to sin as the ultimate source of oppression.

The function of civilization, therefore, is similar to that of the law in that its inadequacies externalize sin as does the inadequacy of legal observance. On the personal, existential level sin is seen as accounting for the futility we experience in attempting to attain life and authenticate our existence through observance of the law, and salvation represents the restoration of human nature's essential goodness. On the cultural, historical level the presence of sin accounts for the fact that the visible, created world is "subjected to futility" (Rom. 8:20; Jerusalem Bible translation: "made unable to attain its purpose"), and salvation refers to the restoration of creation's essential goodness. In the encyclical *Redemptor Hominis* (1979) Pope John Paul II applies St. Paul's phrase precisely to the historical process of civilization, maintaining that reflection on contemporary civilization leads, on the one hand, to an awareness of unprecedented progress but, on the other, to awareness, to a previously unknown degree, of creation's subjection "to futility":

> Does not the previously unknown immense progress—which has taken place especially in the course of this century—in the field of human dominion over the world itself reveal—to a previously unknown degree—that manifold subjection "to futility"? . . . The world of the new age, the world of space flights, the world of the previously unattained conquests of science and technology—is it not also the world "groaning in travail" that "waits with eager longing for the revealing of the children of God"?[31]

As evidence of the world's subjection to futility John Paul points to such baneful side effects of scientific and technological progress as pollution of the environment, war, and the threat of nuclear conflict.

It is this "subjection to futility"—the fact that "things get worse as they get better"—which turns both the law and culture from sources of life into occasions of "death," but a death which is the precondition for that experience of grace and faith which makes life in the form of agape possible. Hence, in another context, Pope John Paul, speaking to the conference of Latin American bishops at Puebla, Mexico, in January 1979, maintains that authentic liberation theology must be based on a uniquely Christian understanding of liberation which goes beyond (though it includes) social, economic, and political liberation. Therefore, it is necessary for the church to avoid being identified with purely secular ideologies in order to avoid being identified completely with the process of civilization—a process which inevitably produces death in the form of guilt—and in order to hold out the promise of a liberation which transcends the limited possibilities of the historical, cultural process.[32]

This shift in theological reflection to the cultural and historical plane also highlights a conviction which, as we have seen, is common to both Christian and Freudian thought, namely, that "life" can only be attained through the historical process of civilization, with its repressions and the guilt it inflicts. Life is not to be found in a regressive movement to the past but by renouncing the past in favour of the future. That future inevitably holds out the prospect of "death" since civilization is a guilt-producing process, but that death is a necessary precondition of life. The kingdom of God—like the Freudian Eros—is a concept which gives meaning to the historical process of civilization; and the meaning it gives to that process is in keeping with the fundamental paradox of Christianity—that one must die in order to live. The "tree of life" is not to be found by a regressive attempt to recapture a paradise lost but by a forward movement which accepts all that is symbolized by the cross. As the prayer of the church proclaims: "In the cross of our Lord is revealed the tree of life."[33]

NOTES

1. Denzinger, *Enchiridion Symbolorum*, 790.
2. The point of the decree on original sin, for example, is that the remission of original sin is only possible through the redemptive work of Christ, which is applied to individuals through the sacrament of baptism. The transmission of the "sin of Adam" is referred to only in the relative clause "quod origine unum est et propagatione non imitatione transfusum omnibus inest" (Denzinger, 790). Likewise, in the same decree, the doctrinal definition of the necessity of infant baptism is followed by an exposition in which the purpose of the church's practice of baptizing infants is explained in the words "ut in eis regeneratione mundetur, quod generatione contraxerunt" (Denzinger, 791).
3. André-Marie Dubarle, *The Biblical Doctrine of Original Sin*, trans. E. M. Stewart (New York: Herder and Herder, 1967).
4. Denzinger, 791.
5. See Brian O. McDermott, S.J., "The Theology of Original Sin: Recent Developments," *Theological Studies* 38.3 (1977): 478–512.
6. Ibid., p. 480.
7. Dubarle, *The Biblical Doctrine of Original Sin*, p. 244.
8. Ibid., p. 241.
9. G. Vandervelde identifies Piet Schoonenberg, Karl Rahner, and Heinz Weger with this situational view. See his *Original Sin: Two Major Trends in Catholic Reinterpretation* (Amsterdam: Rodopi, 1975).

10. Louis Monden, S.J., *Sin, Liberty, and Law*, trans. Joseph Donceel, S.J. (New York: Sheed and Ward, 1965), p. 71.
11. Ibid., p. 72.
12. Sharon MacIsaac, *Freud and Original Sin* (New York: Paulist Press, 1974), p. 115.
13. Ibid., p. 118.
14. Christian Duquoc, "New Approaches to Original Sin," trans. Joe Cuneen, *Cross Currents* Summer 1978: 196.
15. Ibid., p. 196.
16. In this connection it is difficult to overlook the wording of the decree on justification, which insists that individuals contract their own injustice in the event of conception. Men, it insists, born through generation of the seed of Adam, contract through Adam, in conception, injustice as their own [". . . cum ea propagatione per ipsum dum concipiuntur, propriam iniustitiam contrahant . . ." (Denzinger, 795)].
17. Theodore Roszak, *Where the Wasteland Ends* (Garden City, N.Y.: Doubleday, 1972), p. xxiii.
18. Karl Barth, *Epistle to the Romans*, trans. C. Hoskyns (London: Oxford University Press, 1933), p. 242.
19. Erik Erikson, *Childhood and Society* (New York: Norton, 1963), p. 267.
20. Ibid.
21. Paul Tillich, *Systematic Theology*, 3 vols. (Chicago: University of Chicago Press, 1951–1963), 2:29–44. Tillich's view seems to suggest that the essential goodness of human nature is not an existential given but a goal to be achieved through a process of development which includes a redemptive factor by which the state of estrangement from our essential being is overcome. In other words, the essential goodness of human nature represents the goal of human development, but a transcendent goal which is beyond human achievement and can be realized, in the Christian view, only through that grace which is manifest in Christ. To maintain the essential goodness of human nature it is not necessary to believe that goodness is fully actualized from the moment of birth. Like the rest of creation we are "eagerly awaiting" that degree of fulfillment, and we "groan inwardly" since the fulfillment (salvation) we desire is not an accomplished fact but "something we must wait for with patience" (Rom. 8:18–25).
22. *Jerome Biblical Commentary* (Englewood Cliffs, N.J.: Prentice Hall, 1968), 53:77.
23. Stanislas Lyonnet, "St. Paul: Liberty and Law," in *The Bridge: A Yearbook of Judaeo-Christian Studies* (New York: Pantheon Books, 1961), 4:237–38.
24. Karl Barth, *Church Dogmatics* (Edinburgh: T. & T. Clark, 1956), p. 105.

25. Sigmund Freud, *Civilization and Its Discontents*, trans. James Strachey (New York: Norton, 1961), p. 42.
26. Ibid., p. 43.
27. Anders Nygren, *Agape and Eros*, trans. Philip J. Watson (London: SPCK, 1953), p. 129.
28. Sigmund Freud, *An Outline of Psychoanalysis*, trans. James Strachey (New York: Norton, 1949), pp. 20–21.
29. Paul Ricoeur, *Freud and Philosophy: An Essay on Interpretation*, trans. Denis Savage (New Haven: Yale University Press, 1970), pp. 292–93.
30. Freud, *An Outline of Psychoanalysis*, pp. 20–21.
31. *Redemptor Hominis*, March 4, 1979, II, 8.
32. Address to the Third General Assembly of Latin American Bishops at Puebla, Mexico, Jan. 28, 1979, I-4,8,9 and III-2,3,6.
33. Sunday of Week I, Office of Readings, Antiphon I.

JUNG AND CHRISTIANITY

[Christ] intends to complete in us the mysteries of
his incarnation, birth and hidden life by forming
himself in us, being reborn in our souls through
the holy sacraments of baptism and the Eucharist.
                St. John Eudes, *On the Kingdom of Jesus*

Christ would never have made the impression he
did on his followers if he had not expressed something that was alive and at work in their unconscious. Christianity itself would never have spread
through the pagan world with such astonishing
rapidity had its ideas not found an analogous
psychic readiness to receive them. It is this fact
which also makes it possible to say that whoever
believes in Christ is not only contained in him, but
that Christ then dwells in the believer as the perfect man formed in the image of God, the second
Adam.
                Carl Jung, *Answer to Job*

Chapter 4
Faith and Wholeness

AS we have seen, the question posed by contemporary natural theology is not "Does God exist?" but "Why is the human person religious?" In addressing this question to Freudian theory we have identified the conflict between Eros and the death instinct and the attempt to bring about the victory of Eros over death in individual and social life as dimensions of human existence which correlate with the theological and religious realities of God, sin, grace, and redemption. In the analytical psychology of Carl Jung (1875–1961) the answer to the question of natural theology is to be found in Jung's concept of the "archetypes of the collective unconscious," which, when projected onto religious realities, render them "psychologically real" and therefore meaningful for human existence. For Jung, the human meaning of religious dogma, ritual, myth, and symbol is to be found in their relationship to those archetypal motifs which, as structural components of the "collective unconscious," represent the transpersonal goal and meaning of human existence.

Jung's evaluation of religion is therefore rooted in his understanding of the nature of the unconscious. Jung agreed with Freud in looking upon dreams as a source of information about the unconscious. For Jung, however, the unconscious was not simply a reservoir of repressed personal experiences (the personal unconscious); it was also a storehouse of latent memories and images which the individual inherits from the past history of the human race. What Jolande Jacobi calls "humanity's typical forms of reaction"[1]— those experiences which are repeated in every generation, such as God and religion, the relationship of the sexes, good and evil, motherhood, heroic conflict, birth and death—leave their residue upon the individual psyche, so that each individual is born with a predisposition to see reality in a certain way and to renew and relive these typical experiences of the race. This dimension of the psyche Jung called the "collective unconscious" since it was derived, not from personal experience, but from the collective experience of humanity, containing, in Jung's words, "the whole spiritual heritage of mankind's evolution, born anew in the brain structure of every individual."[2]

To these structural components of the collective unconscious Jung gave the name "archetypes." The archetypes are pre-existent to individual consciousness and are transpersonal, the common possession of humankind, the residue of the repeated experiences of humanity, and they tend towards the repetition of these experiences (*CW*, 7:109). Since these experiences can be healing and growth-producing, the contents of the unconscious are regarded not simply as repressed sources of neurotic symptoms, but also as sources of wisdom and meaning which, when assimilated by consciousness, are expressed in the form of images, symbols, and myths. For Jung, therefore, the archetypes represent potentialities for expressing meaning in myth and symbol, which are seen as conscious representations of unconscious motifs or archetypes. The archetypes therefore are form without content; they are given concrete content by the symbols, myths, rituals, etc., onto which they are projected. Jung describes the archetype as a "structure whose form is not yet determinable but which is endowed with the faculty of appearing in definite forms by way of projection" (*CW*, 9[1]: 142). Consciousness, then, has for Jung a twofold function since it stands between the objective reality of the external world and what is for Jung the equally objective reality (since it is not merely the creation of consciousness) of the inner world of the collective unconscious. The function of consciousness is not only to assimilate external reality but "to translate into visible reality the world within us" (*CW*, 8:342).

This process of translating the inner unconscious world of archetypes into conscious attitudes and behaviour, the "individuation process," was necessary in Jung's view because the conscious ego, left to its own devices, pursues a one-sided path of development; namely, one of adjustment to one's social environment, so that only those aspects of oneself which are perceived as socially acceptable (the "persona") are given conscious expression. The unadapted side of personality (the "shadow") is repressed. When this happens, the unconscious tries to resolve the tension which results from this repression of part of one's total personality by breaking through into consciousness, usually in the form of dreams or phantasies, in order to redirect the growth of personality towards its proper goal of wholeness. This tendency of the unconscious to direct the growth of personality towards the goal of wholeness or selfhood, a tendency which Jung does not hesitate to call "religious," is autonomous, or independent of the conscious ego.

Of all the archetypes of the collective unconscious "the self," the archetype of wholeness, represents the ultimate goal of the individuation process. This quest for wholeness, for the reconciliation of the conscious adapted aspects of one's personality with the unconscious unadapted aspects—what Jung calls the *"coniunctio oppositorum"*—is a "religious" desire for rebirth; or, to put it more accurately, the religious image of rebirth is a conscious symbol of the unconscious quest for wholeness—a conscious representation onto which the archetype of the self is projected. Likewise, the God-image has a similar function; it is a conscious symbol representing the archetype of wholeness or totality. Thus, for Jung, God is "psychologically real" since the God-image, as a symbol of totality, "is immediately related to, or identical with, the self, and everything that happens to the God-image has an effect on the latter" (*CW*, 9[2]:170).

"To be whole," writes Frieda Fordham, "means to become reconciled with those sides of personality which have not been taken into account."[3] This is the goal of the individuation process, which Jung defines as "the process by which a person becomes a psychological 'in-dividual,' that is, a separate, indivisible unity or whole" (*CW*, 9[1]:490). This process of assimilating the unconscious aspects of one's total personality is likened by Jung to the rediscovery of one's soul, since one is thereby recalled to the emotional, instinctive, unconscious sources of motivation and knowledge, and the personality whose growth may have been over-developed in one direction is redirected to the proper goal of wholeness. Here again is reflected Jung's understanding of the unconscious as a source of meaning and value for human existence. Erich Fromm has suggested that Freud, the rationalist, arrived at an understanding of the unconscious which "was based on his wish to control and subdue it," while Jung, the romantic anti-rationalist, saw the non-rational unconscious as "the deepest source of wisdom." He concludes: "Jung's interest in the unconscious was the admiring one of the romantic; Freud's the critical one of the rationalist."[4]

We should note, to begin with, two features of the individ-

uation process: (1) The assimilation of unconscious contents is normally the developmental task of the second half of life. In the first
half of life the conscious ego's primary concern is that of adaptation to the demands of external reality. The questions of personal
identity, career, marriage, and family are uppermost. The task of
the second half of life is that of adaptation to the inner world of
the psyche. The "mid-life crisis" is a signal that the values of youth,
with their one-sided emphasis on adaptation to the external world,
are to be abandoned, and new meaning and purpose are to be found
in the assimilation of those very aspects of one's personality which
were repressed, neglected, or underdeveloped during the first half
of life. (2) The process of individuation involves a successive
encountering of the archetypal contents of the unconscious, which
are projected onto those images and symbols encountered in dreams
and phantasies. Jung laid special emphasis on the following
archetypes.

1. The Experience of the Shadow   The shadow, as we have
seen, is the counterpart of the persona, which is the adapted side
of one's personality and therefore the face one shows to the world.
The shadow, the unadapted side of one's personality, represents,
in Jung's words, "everything that the subject refuses to acknowledge
about himself and yet is always thrusting itself upon him directly
or indirectly" (*CW*, 9[1]:513). As the personification of, among
other things, the human propensity to and capacity for evil, the
shadow is repressed because it is incompatible with one's persona,
that is, with one's conscious moral and ethical principles. But this,
argues Jung, leads to an artificial, one-sided personality. "Whoever," he states, "builds up too good a persona for himself naturally
has to pay for it with irritability" (*CW*, 7:306). To deny the dark
side of one's personality is to deny a part of one's total self, and,
as Jung maintains, "a man cannot get rid of himself in favour of
an artificial personality without punishment" (*CW*, 7:307).

2. The Encounter with the Anima/Animus   The anima/
animus archetype represents the contrasexual side of the psyche
and is experienced in the same way as the shadow; that is, in others
through projection. The anima, the feminine side of the masculine
personality, is encountered, through projection, in one's wife,
mother, etc., while the animus, the masculine side of the feminine
personality, is encountered, again through projection, in one's
husband, father, etc. In the course of development consciousness

differentiates between masculine and feminine and identifies with one of the opposites. The contrasexual side of one's personality is relegated to the unconscious and projected onto the opposite sex. In the interests of wholeness the projection must be withdrawn and the unconscious content assimilated. Hence Jung refers to the recognition of the anima/animus as the mediating function between the ego and the inner world of the psyche, just as the persona mediates between the ego and the outer world. The persona represents one's habitual external attitude; the anima/animus, one's habitual, inner, unconscious attitude. It is the opposite of the persona, as is the shadow.

3. The Self   The archetype of the self represents, as we have seen, the goal of the individuation process. It is the archetype of wholeness, unity, and totality. As such, it is the archetype most closely related to the central question of natural theology, for in Jung's opinion it is this archetype which is projected onto the various God-images appearing throughout the history of religion, and which therefore makes those God-images meaningful for human existence.

It is in the context of Jung's understanding of the individuation process that we can appreciate his evaluation of the symbolic language of religion. Since individuation is a process in which unconscious contents are encountered and assimilated into consciousness by being projected onto archetypal symbols, perhaps we can arrive at a deeper understanding of certain Christian sacramental symbols by interpreting them as archetypal symbols within the context of the individuation process. In other words, we can enquire whether a correlation exists between the human quest for wholeness or selfhood and the symbols which are operative in the liturgical and sacramental life of the church. In our present context this is the question of natural theology. Religious symbols are seen by Jung as "symbols of transformation" which direct the libido or psychic energy towards the psychological and religious goal of selfhood. This can best be illustrated, perhaps, with reference to his interpretation of the Oedipus complex for, in Jung's view, the incestuous desire attributed to the child at this stage of growth is in reality a desire for rebirth. Freud had described the function of the incest taboo as the prevention of incest and the turning of the child's sexual libido away from the parental figure and towards other objects, which are therefore seen as essentially substitute objects. Other love objects, therefore, including religious objects, remain to some extent substitutes for the original object of the sexual libido—symbols, in effect, of our most fundamental but unfulfilled desire.

Victor White has pointed out that Jung reverses this interpretation of the Oedipus complex by maintaining that the incestuous wish is not the thing symbolised by other desires but is itself a symbol of a more fundamental desire—the desire for rebirth:

> Impregnation of the mother for its own sake, or motivated by the pleasure principle, was not the ultimate object of the libido at all; what was really desired was the return to the womb—rebirth. The incest wish is no longer the ultimate "thing symbolised"; it is itself the symbol of a yet more fundamental need and desire. Hence it could be that manifest sexuality is itself symbolic; it is in fact only one form of life-urge bigger than itself.[5]

In this view, therefore, religion is not a substitute for the desired mother; the desire for the mother is a symbol for what one really wants—rebirth through return to the mother's womb. The incestuous desire is in reality symbolic of a religious and spiritual desire for rebirth which cannot be accomplished by a mere return to the womb. It was this truth which Jesus tried to impress upon Nicodemus (John 3:1-8), who understood Jesus' words about being "born again" in a purely naturalistic way.

Jesus uses the notion of the wind which "blows wherever it pleases" as symbolic of the activity of the Spirit in order to raise Nicodemus' mind to an appreciation of the reality of spiritual rebirth. Jung notes that this is the function of symbols which "act as *transformers*, their function being to convert libido from a 'lower' into a 'higher' form" (*CW*, 5:344). The incest prohibition, therefore, does not simply have the purpose of preventing actual incest; it also "makes the creative fantasy inventive" (*CW*, 5:332); that is, it creates the possibility of redirecting the libido towards the goal of spiritual and psychological rebirth through its response to myth and symbol. This is the function of myths and symbols of the mother and of rebirth; they canalize psychic energy away from the actual physical mother and onto mother analogies or symbols of the mother, so that the aim of the libido is "spiritualized":

Moreover it must be pointed out that the basis of the
"incestuous" desire is not cohabitation, but, as every
sun myth shows, the strange idea of becoming a child
again, of returning to the parental shelter, and of
entering into the mother in order to be reborn through
her. But the way to this goal lies through incest, i.e.,
the necessity of finding some way into the mother's
body. One of the simplest ways would be to impregnate the mother and beget oneself in identical form
all over again. But here the incest prohibition inter-
venes; consequently the sun myths and rebirth myths
devise every conceivable kind of mother-analogy for
the purpose of canalizing the libido into new forms
and effectively preventing it from regressing to actual
incest. . . . It is not incestuous cohabitation that is
desired, but rebirth. (*CW*, 5:332)

The effect of the incest taboo is to create the possibility for canalizing the libido away from actual incest and towards the goal of
rebirth. "In this way," Jung states, "the libido becomes imper-
ceptibly spiritualized . . . . That is why the religions exalt this
procedure into a system" (*CW*, 5:332).

Put in general terms, Jung's interpretation points to the
human desire to return to union with the lost part of one's personality—its unconscious depths—for the sake of wholeness or completeness. This desire is symbolized by the incestuous desire for
the mother—a symbol of the unconscious. But the incestuous desire
is a regressive "psychic danger." Hence the incest taboo "opposes
the libido and blocks the path to regression," thus making it possible
for the libido to be canalized into the "mother analogies thrown
up by the unconscious" (*CW*, 5:313). The mother analogies are
symbols of rebirth, and rebirth implies a radical transformation
which cannot be brought about merely by an act of the will. It can
only be brought about by redirecting the psychic energy which
desires the return to the mother towards mother analogies. "No
man," Jung argues, "can change himself into anything from sheer
reason; he can only change into what he potentially is. When such
a change becomes necessary, the previous mode of adaptation,
already in a state of decay, is unconsciously compensated by the
archetype of another mode" (*CW*, 5:351). The archetypes repre-

sent the unconscious potentialities of the psyche; rebirth involves the actualizing of these unconscious potentialities by redirecting the energy of the psyche towards the archetypal goals. "Born again" Christians typically reject such psychological explanations, which nevertheless can be put forward without calling into question the religious or theological interpretation of the experience or the faith of the believer.

It is in this context that Jung sees much of the symbolism of religion and mythology as mother analogies and, therefore, symbols of rebirth. The ancient sun myths, for example, which describe the "death" of the sun through immersion in the sea and its "rebirth" after its mysterious night journey in the depths of the sea, are mythical expressions of the desire for rebirth by return- ing to the womb (the sea). "The meaning of this cycle of myths," Jung maintains, "is clear enough; it is the longing to attain rebirth through a return to the womb, and to become immortal like the sun" (CW, 5:312). As can be seen from this type of myth, water is symbolic of the mother, and a large body of water (the sea), of the unconscious. Rebirth is by way of reimmersion in the uncon- scious, which is the source or matrix of conscious life. Consequently "the unconscious when interpreted on the subjective level, has the same maternal significance as water" (CW, 5:320).

In the context of our present discussion the religious symbol- ism we are primarily concerned with is the sacramental symbolism of the Christian liturgy. In this regard the question of natural theol- ogy would be: Do these sacramental signs, which are an integral part of the Christian's life of prayer and worship, relate meaning- fully to human existence? The Jungian answer to this question would identify the Christian sacramental signs as "symbols of trans- formation"; that is, as symbols of rebirth which direct psychic energy towards the goal of selfhood. The church has traditionally used the word *sign* in reference to the sacraments since they are visible signs which recall and celebrate the mystery of grace and redemption.

The teaching of the church, however, defines sacraments not merely as empty signs conveying information or recalling an event, but as "effective signs of grace" making present in some way the reality they signify. It is precisely because they are "effective" signs that sacraments can be thought of as symbols as Jung understands the term. For Jung, a sign was a rationally composed representation of something real and definite, so that it can be translated into words, communicating information. A symbol, on the other hand, is a sign which cannot adequately be expressed otherwise. It does not simply convey information but communicates power by reconciling opposites (the transcendent function) and directing psychic energy towards the goal of selfhood. The symbol, as we have seen, has the power to redirect psychic energy towards necessary goals in a way that is beyond the power of reason or willpower. Frieda Fordham states: "In the course of time we have succeeded in detaching a certain proportion of energy from instinct and have also developed the will, but it is less powerful than we like to believe, and we still have need of the transmuting power of the symbol."[6] The Catholic formula which expresses this transmuting power of the sacramental symbol states that the sacraments have an *ex opere operato* effect on the believing recipient; that is, the power of the sacrament is in the sign itself apart from the worthiness or unworthiness of the minister. Jung, I believe, comes close to explaining the psychological dynamics underlying the human experience behind this theological formula in the following statement about symbols:

> The symbol works by suggestion; that is to say, it carries conviction and at the same time expresses the content of that conviction. It is able to do this because of the numen, the specific energy stored up in the archetype. Experience of the archetype is not only impressive, it seizes and possesses the whole personality and is naturally productive of faith. (*CW*, 5:344)

Such a psychological explanation in no way denies the truth of the theological formula; on the contrary, by pointing to the human experience to which the theological teaching refers, it guards against a purely "magical" interpretation of that formula. It also underscores Jung's conviction that genuine faith must be based on experience; that is to say, doctrine must relate meaningfully to the experience of the believer and, in Jungian terms, to the archetypal structures of the human psyche. Otherwise, "the traditional contents gradually lose their real meaning and are only believed in as formalities, without this belief having any influence on the conduct of life. There is no longer a living power behind it (*CW*, 5:345). Jung believed that the efficacy of religion lay in the symbolic character of its message. Religion represented a symbol onto which the archetypal content of the psyche—the human desire for rebirth—could be projected. "The reason," he argues, "why Jesus' words have such great suggestive power is that they express the symbolical truths which are rooted in the very structure of the human psyche" (*CW*, 5:335). Without denying that the sacraments are effective signs containing the reality they signify, could we not suggest that they are effective in the sense of bringing about real change in human personality to the extent that they are symbolic of the archetypal contents of the human psyche? It is from this perspective that we shall briefly examine the sacraments of baptism and the Eucharist.

The theme of rebirth which baptism symbolizes is, of course, central to Christianity. Paul Tillich has described this experience of rebirth as the overcoming of separation and reunion with the ground of one's being—language which is reminiscent of Jung's description of the rebirth imagery as symbolic of the reunion of consciousness with its unconscious depths. In his famous sermon "You Are Accepted,"[7] Tillich tries to make the terms *sin* and *grace* meaningful by relating them to the experiences of separation and reconciliation which characterize human existence. "Existence is separation," he declares—separation from oneself, from one's fellow human beings, and ultimately from the ground of all being—and it is this state of separation that is referred to by the word *sin*. The awareness of God comes with the experience of reunion or reconciliation by which this separation is overcome. The religious word for this experience of reunion is *grace*, because it is the result of being accepted and affirmed by the ground or power of being and is therefore beyond our power to control. As we saw in chapter 1, Tillich speaks of the self-transcending quality of human existence by which it "points beyond itself." More precisely, it is this separated, alienated condition of human existence which points to a state of reunion and reconciliation, which Tillich refers to as the "new being."

In Jungian theory, this separated and alienated quality of human existence is attributed to the growth of consciousness, which, as we have seen, implies separation from one's unconscious depths and therefore from the deepest sources of life and wisdom. Both analyses of human existence can be expressed mythically in the biblical story of the fall and the expulsion from paradise. Whether the mode of expression is mythical, theological, or psychological, the same fundamental truth emerges: human persons, in the actual conditions of their existence, stand in need of rebirth, redemption, and reconciliation. This is the goal of both psychological and religious growth, and religious symbols, therefore, direct the energy of the psyche towards a goal or telos which is at the same time the goal of psychological growth.

This means that the sacramental symbolism of rebirth in baptism has a psychological meaning which in no way contradicts its theological meaning. We have already seen that in Jung's interpretation of the Oedipus complex, the function of the incest taboo is to deflect the incestuous desire towards a desire for spiritual rebirth (symbolized by reunion with the mother) by substituting for the physical mother symbols which are mother analogies. In this way the incestuous desire is "spiritualized," but it is the same energy which is represented by the incestuous wish which is transformed and used in the pursuit of this spiritual and psychological goal of rebirth.

The pursuit of rebirth or selfhood is an arduous task which, for Jung, was represented mythically by the archetypal figure of the hero. The hero myth is "an unconscious drama seen only in projection" (CW, 5:612). The hero figure's quest, his search for the beloved, represents a search for the mother, which is in turn symbolic of a search for unconscious contents or "unlived life." The whole process of individuation is reflected in the hero's separation from the mother (growth of consciousness and separation from unconscious) and his quest to be reunited with her (reassimilation of unconscious contents). The hero's quest is a regression to the mother, but "the regression leads back only apparently to the mother; in reality she is the gateway into the unconscious" (CW, 5:508). The mother, therefore, must be rediscovered in a symbolic, that is, non-incestuous form since it is a search for rebirth. To emphasize the goal of rebirth the hero's birth takes place under extraordinary circumstances, or the hero has two mothers (being reared by foster parents). The hero, says Jung, "is not born like an ordinary mortal because his birth is a rebirth" (CW, 5:494).

Instead of having two mothers, the hero may experience two births. Jung sees the liturgy of baptism as representing this type of rebirth. The Christian who is born in the normal manner is reborn like the hero in the womb of mother church. "Man is not

merely born in the commonplace sense, but is born again in a
mysterious manner, and so partakes of divinity. Anyone who is
reborn in this way becomes a hero, a semi-divine being" (*CW*,
5:494). The notion of rebirth is strikingly symbolized in the Easter
liturgy. In the Easter Vigil service the liturgy of baptism begins
with a prayer that God will bless the baptismal font "that those
reborn in it may be made one with his adopted children in Christ."
The prayer for the blessing of the baptismal water begins by enunciating the principle that the grace of God is communicated through
sacramental signs "which tell us of the wonders of your unseen
power." There then follows a recitation of the various ways in which
water was seen as symbolic of God's life-giving powers in the biblical
narrative: the Spirit breathing on the waters in the divine act of
creation; the waters of the flood which marked "an end of sin and
a new beginning of goodness"; the rescue of the Israelites through
the waters of the Red Sea, "an image of God's holy people set free
from sin by baptism"; the baptism of Jesus in the waters of the
Jordan; the flow of water and blood from the wounded side of Christ
on the cross. The Easter candle—a symbol of Christ—is then
lowered into the baptismal water so as to impregnate, as it were,
and make fruitful the font (the womb of mother church) that it might
bring forth, through rebirth, children of God. The font, the baptismal water, and the church itself are what Jung would call "mother
analogies," which relate meaningfully to the archetypal theme of
rebirth in the human psyche. Jung also points out that Christ's
death on the cross was understood as a rebirth since the cross, like
the tree from which it is made, is symbolic of mother and of life.
Hence the cross of Jesus is in reality the tree of life—an instrument of death and rebirth. Christ refers to his coming crucifixion
as a "baptism": "There is a baptism I must still receive, and how
great is my distress till it is over" (Luke 12:50). This theme of death
and rebirth is symbolized more explicitly in baptism by immersion,
which symbolizes being buried with Christ and rising to a new life
with him. But even without the rite of immersion the same meaning
of death and rebirth is attached to the baptismal rite as we can see,
again, with reference to the rite of blessing the baptismal water.
The priest, holding the Easter candle, which represents Christ, in
the baptismal water, prays: "May all who are buried with Christ
in the death of baptism rise also with him to newness of life." If,
for Jung, rebirth refers to the achieving of a higher state of con-

sciousness through assimilation of unconscious contents, then the death which precedes rebirth refers to the sacrifice of one's one-sided conscious attitudes for the sake of wholeness. Here again it would appear that Jung has interpreted a psychic phenomenon, the death wish—which Freud saw as fundamental and irreducible— as symbolic of a deeper desire, the desire for rebirth. Consciousness experiences a "death" through reimmersion in the unconscious, but, like the Christian being buried with Christ in baptism, it is for the sake of rebirth. Jung claims that this "death" is often represented in dreams and phantasies as death in the form of an arrow-shot inflicted by another. But the arrow is really one's own unconscious demanding a new psychic adaptation. "That the highest summit of life," Jung writes, "can be expressed through the symbolism of death is a well-known fact, for any growing beyond oneself means death" (CW, 5:432).

Jung also finds the liturgy of the Eucharist symbolic of this kind of psychological death and rebirth. In his essay "Transformation Symbolism in the Mass" he speaks of transubstantiation as an "absolute impossibility" from the rational standpoint and asks this question: "What is it that induces us to represent an absolute impossibility? What is it that for thousands of years has wrung from man the greatest spiritual effort, the loveliest works of art, the profoundest devotion, the most heroic self-sacrifice, and the most exacting service?" (CW, 11:379). The religious answer to this question would be "faith" and it would be correct; but Jung's assertion that genuine faith rests on and is related to experience is equally correct. Hence, for Jung, the answer to his question is that the symbolic representation of this "absolute impossibility" is the result of a "miracle": "It is a miracle which is not man's to command; for as soon as he tries to work it himself, or as soon as he philosophizes about it and tries to comprehend it intellectually, the bird is flown. A miracle is something that arouses man's wonder precisely because it seems inexplicable" (CW, 11:379). For Jung, what lies behind this inexplicable miracle and our faith in it is the activity of the unconscious self, which he cites in explaining both the symbolic and sacrificial qualities of the rite.

1. Eucharist as Symbolic   The presence of Christ in the Eucharist, which is the object of the believer's faith, does not refer simply to his reappearance, nor is the consecration of the mass merely the repetition of an historical event. In the teaching of the

church it is a re-presentation of a once-and-for-all event of redemption, a sign of what the believer sees as God's eternal redeeming
love. Jung, therefore, describes it as "the revelation of something
existing in eternity, a rending of the veil of temporal and spatial
limitations which separates the human spirit from the sight of the
eternal" (*CW*, 11:307). The rite is therefore symbolic rather than
a mere sign. A sign stands for a "known and conceivable fact,"
whereas a symbol is an "only partly valid" expression of something which is only "partly conceivable," that is, of something
beyond rational conception—a mystery (*CW*, 11:307). In psychological terms what lies beyond the limits of rational consciousness
is the unconscious. It is an unconscious truth—a mystery—which
is expressed in the Eucharist. Such a truth can only be expressed
symbolically. This, for Jung, is true of all deeply rooted religious
beliefs. The authority behind such beliefs is not only the authority
of faith but also the authority of the unconscious self. It is for this
reason that they are not just rationally constructed beliefs subject
to rational correction. Because such beliefs rest on an authority
beyond rational consciousness, Jung can say: "An improbable
opinion has to submit sooner or later to correction. But the statements of religion are the most improbable of all and yet they persist
for thousands of years" (*CW*, 11:379).

2. Eucharist as Sacrifice   In church teaching there are two
aspects to the Eucharist; it is both a sacrifice and a meal—a representation of both the sacrifice of the cross and the last supper, the
Passover sacrifice and the Passover meal. The Catholic liturgical
renewal of recent years has rightly reintroduced the word *celebration*
in reference to participation in the Eucharistic liturgy, but in practice
the word is sometimes used in such a way as to obscure the fact
that it is precisely the redemptive sacrifice of Christ that one is cele-
brating. What Jung has to say, therefore, about the psychological
meaning of the Eucharist might prove salutary since the focus of
his interest is most particularly the mass as a sacrifice.

     Jung emphasizes the fact that sacrifice refers to the giving
of a gift, but the gift giving in this case has a special character.
In ordinary gift giving there is a conscious or unconscious expectation of receiving something in return—even if only in the form
of the goodwill or gratitude of the recipient. In sacrifice, however,
the gift is given without expectation of anything in return. It is
this egoistic expectation which must be renounced in sacrifice.

Moreover, since the gift represents the giver, the gift of self must also be free of any egoistic claim. "It only becomes a sacrifice," says Jung, "if I give up the implied intention of receiving something in return. If it is to be a true sacrifice, the gift must be given as if it were being destroyed. Only then is it possible for the egoistic claim to be given up" (*CW*, 11:390). In order to do this, it is necessary for the giver to come to an awareness of his identity with the gift and of sacrificing that part of himself which is identical with the gift. In other words, one must become conscious of the egoistic claim and renounce it: "The conscious realization of this alone guarantees that the giving is a real sacrifice. For if I know and admit that I am giving myself, forgoing myself, and do not want to be repaid for it, then I have sacrificed my claim, and thus a part of myself" (*CW*, 11:390).

This intentional loss or sacrifice of the ego, however, is also a gain, for "if you can give yourself it proves that you possess yourself" (*CW*, 11:390). It is in this context that Jung interprets the Eucharist in terms of the theme of psychological death and rebirth and interprets the sacrificial aspect of the rite in terms of the activity of the unconscious. For Jung the sacrifice of the ego we have been discussing is psychologically possible because "the ego is a relative quantity which can be subsumed under various superordinate authorities" (*CW*, 11:390). These authorities are not to be equated with the collective moral consciousness (the Freudian superego) or public opinion but with "certain psychic conditions which existed in man from the beginning and are not acquired by experience" (*CW*, 11:390), namely the archetypes of the collective unconscious. The ego, therefore, does not represent the total personality; rather, it is possible "for a more compendious personality to emerge in the course of development and take the ego into its service" (*CW*, 11:390). This more compendious personality is what Jung calls the self—the total personality which represents the union of conscious and unconscious contents. Psychologically, it is for the sake of the self that the ego is sacrificed. The sacrifice of the Eucharist expresses in a symbolic way this desire for self-sacrifice, which is in reality a desire for rebirth to a higher level of consciousness, just as Christ's sacrifice was a rebirth to a new life.

By way of a corollary to our discussion of the Eucharist, a word should be said about the Catholic sacrament of penance or reconciliation, for it relates intimately to the Eucharist and also to Jung's concept of the "shadow," or dark side of personality, and the reconciliation of good and evil.

Jung's rejection of Freud's exclusively sexual interpretation of the term *libido* made him more acceptable to Catholic thinkers in particular. Unfortunately, however, his own interpretation of the term also creates a problem for those interested in the integration of Jungian and Christian thought. "Libido" for Jung is the energy created by the conflict of opposites. Life is a dynamic tension created by the struggle of contending forces. This law of opposites (Heraclitus' law of enantiodromia) includes the opposites of good and evil. Since the goal of human growth is the harmonious "union of opposites," then—contrary to our conventional notions of morality—a way must be found, not to eliminate evil, but to effect a reconciliation of the good and evil aspects of personality.

This "evil" aspect of personality is conceptualized by Jung as the "shadow" archetype. The dark side of personality, its potentiality for evil, is kept in suppression because it contradicts our conscious principles. Hence one aspect of the conflict of opposites within the psyche is this conflict between the conscious pursuit of the good and the unconscious tendency to evil. One aspect of the individual's growth in consciousness is the development of conscience, that is, of conscious moral principles which the individual strives to live up to, as to an image or ideal expressive of his own and society's expectations. Accordingly, those aspects of one's personality which are at variance with the ideal must be kept in suppression and thus become the "dark side" of personality, which nevertheless, according to Jung's notion of the self-regulating nature of the psyche, continues to seek conscious expression in order to achieve a balance or union of opposites.

Thus the conscious moral personality which we present to society in response to its moral demands (the "persona" in Jung's terms) is built up at the expense of the dark side of personality, and the more this dark side is repressed the more it tends to express itself in negative and destructive ways, a principle which Jung applied to any repressed or neglected part of one's personality. We invariably pay a price for one-sided development. Now if the sacrament of penance has become an inauthentic sign of grace for many and even psychologically damaging for some, it is, I believe, because the practice of confession has become in many instances an attempt to "get rid of oneself in favour of an artificial personality." Perhaps the emphasis placed on the "purpose of amendment" deluded penitents into believing that by force of willpower they could eliminate the dark side of personality and conform to the conscious ideal image of themselves. But to identify completely with one's persona is to identify with only part of oneself. Moral perfection is thus pursued at the expense of psychic wholeness or completeness, and that self-knowledge which should be one of the principal fruits of confession is frustrated through the inability to really perceive one's weaknesses.

The experience of St. Paul, which is prototypical for all Christians, is that sin cannot be eradicated from human nature but must be submitted to the grace of God; that the believer does not become acceptable to God by making himself acceptable but by the gratuitous act of God in accepting him, in the words of Paul Tillich, "in spite of being unacceptable."[8] Such acceptance on God's part makes possible for the believer a degree of self-acceptance, which in turn brings one's tendency to evil under greater conscious control since it is now consciously accepted as part of oneself. Thus faith is seen as that which makes possible what Jung considers a psychological necessity—the conscious acceptance of one's total self, including the shadow or dark side of personality. If the sacramental sign of penance has become obscured, it is perhaps because in too many instances the penitent approaches the sacrament as a "beginning again," an exercise in self-improvement by which he hopes to make himself acceptable to his God, rather than as an exercise in faith by which he exposes himself to divine mercy, which accepts him in spite of his inability to eliminate the dark side of his personality. The "healthy" (i.e., those who are unaware of their unhealthy condition) have no need of a physician. In the same way, the sacramental sign of penance is lost on the penitent who does not accept the dark side of personality as part of his total self, thereby turning what should be a renewal of faith in God's forgiving and reconciling love into a renewal of belief in the self-sufficiency of one's idealized self.

It is at this point that the connection between confession and community becomes more apparent, for it is through the confession of sin that the penitent maintains an awareness of his sin and guilt (his shadow) and in the experience of forgiveness that he learns to accept this dark side as part of himself, that is, to accept his total self. Charles Hanna states:

> The primary purpose of confession is to keep people
> aware of their true condition, of the tension between
> the good and evil in themselves. . . . The most
> dangerous thing that can happen to us is that we
> become unaware of, or unconscious of, our sin and
> guilt.[9]

Not only is such unconsciousness of evil dangerous to the individual,
it is, in Jung's view, destructive of community; for whatever is not
accepted as part of one's own personality is projected onto others.
In Jung's view, if we do not recognize the evil in ourselves, we
lose the capacity to deal with it. Since rational consciousness operates
on an idealized image of itself, it is preoccupied with preserving
that image. Accordingly, it protects itself from all attacks on its
self-esteem by indulging in self-justifying projections. Evil is not
attributed to oneself; it is always projected onto others. We are all
familiar enough with the tendency to see evil as always originating
in some outside source, whether it be the younger generation or
the older generation, communist conspiracy or bourgeois decadence.
It is this tendency which Christ contradicted when he affirmed that
it is "not what goes into the mouth that defiles a man, but what
comes out of the mouth" (Matt. 15:11). The source of evil thoughts,
murder, adultery, etc., is placed not in social environmental conditions but in the human heart (Matt. 15:18–20).

    For Jung, what ultimately destroys human community is the
individual's tendency to believe that his true self coincides with
the ideal self manufactured by the ego, and thus his failing to recognize the evil in himself since that ideal image can only be preserved
by projecting evil onto others:

> Since it is universally believed that man is merely what
> his consciousness knows of itself, he regards himself
> as harmless and so adds stupidity to his iniquity. He
> does not deny that terrible things have happened and
> will go on happening, but it is always "the others"
> who do them. . . . It would be an insufferable thought
> that we had to take personal responsibility for so much
> guiltiness. We therefore prefer to localize the evil with
> individual criminals or groups of criminals, while
> washing our hands in innocence and ignoring the
> general proclivity to evil. (*CW*, 10:572–73)

The transcending of this kind of ego-defensiveness can only come about through the recognition and acceptance of the shadow—the dark side of one's personality. When one recognizes that the evil in the world is also within oneself, then defensiveness and self-justifying projections are given up. Moreover, the ego is transcended in another sense; for with the recognition of the "shadow" in one-self, the need for projection disappears, and one is able to relate to others as equals rather than from a position of superiority or defensiveness. Intersubjectivity becomes possible, and not only egoism but narcissism and isolation are transcended. Jung contends that human relationships become possible when individuals achieve the modesty and ability to acknowledge imperfection, which comes with the recognition of the "shadow":

> Recognition of the shadow, on the other hand, leads to the modesty we need in order to acknowledge imperfection. . . . The perfect has no need of the other, but weakness has, for it seeks support and does not confront its partner with anything that might force him into an inferior position and even humiliate him. This humiliation may happen only too easily where idealism plays too prominent a role. (*CW*, 10:579)

Translating all of this into a more Christian vocabulary, we might suggest that it is not so much sin as such but sin which is unrecognized, repressed, unconfessed which is the true obstacle to Christian community; for sin and guilt which are not consciously recognized as one's own are attributed (projected) to others. The other then becomes a source of evil against whom one must protect oneself by erecting defensive barriers. Hence the central importance given to the necessity of repentance in the Christian message, for repentance involves precisely that recognition of sin and guilt (the "shadow") and withdrawal of enmity-creating projections which are necessary for creating the community that is a sign of God's kingdom. There is no such thing as "instant community." It can only be achieved by entering through the "narrow gate" of repentance. Naïve idealism which ignores the dark side of human existence can, in the end, be destructive of genuine community. The traditional Christian understanding is that the bond which unites the Christian community is not the realization that we are self-actualizers, but that in the first instance we are a community of sinners. If the sacrament of penance is to regain its position in the life of that community, perhaps it is time to realize that ultimately the quality of the individual's repentance provides the basis for community.

If the Eucharist is *the* sacrament of reconciliation, what is the function of penance in relation to it? This relationship of penance to Eucharist is not just the result of theological speculation: it was, until recent years, part and parcel of the Catholic mentality. For generations of Catholics, this meant that the reception of communion was regularly preceded by the confession of sins. A good confession made one "worthy" to receive communion. I submit that although the nature of the relationship was painfully distorted, the Catholic laity were demonstrating a certain intuition of faith in seeing an appropriateness in the confession of sins before participation in the Eucharist. There is no greater witness to the truth that penance finds its truest meaning only in relation to the Eucharist, than the fact that the majority of Catholics, having been disabused of the notion that confession was a necessary precondition for reception of the Eucharist, have simply stopped confessing with any frequency.

I believe that the current neglect of the sacrament results from the fact that when unrelated to the Eucharist, it loses its deepest meaning. Thus the theological and pastoral task would seem to be to discover the proper basis on which penance can be related to the Eucharist. Here again, I believe, Jung has a contribution to make to the discussion.

As we have seen, in the essay "Transformation Symbolism in the Mass" Jung offers a useful analysis of the psychology of sacrifice. To offer a gift is to offer oneself, and to offer a sacrifice is to offer oneself without the expectation of receiving something in return. In order to offer a true sacrifice, therefore, one must become consciously aware of the presence of the egoistic claim bound up in every gift in order to consciously give it up:

> One ought to realize that when one gives or surrenders oneself there are corresponding claims attached, the more so, the less one knows of them. The conscious realization of this alone guarantees that the giving is a real sacrifice. (*CW*, 11:390)

It is here that Jung locates the function of confession in relation to the Eucharist. This sacrificing of oneself and one's egoistic claims, he states, "presupposes an act of considerable self-knowledge, lacking which one remains permanently unconscious of such claims" (*CW*, 11:390). The self-examination involved in the confession of sins is intended to make the penitent conscious of such egoistic claims:

> It is therefore quite logical that the confession of sin should come before the rite of transformation in the Mass. The self-examination is intended to make one conscious of the selfish claim bound up with every gift so that it may be consciously given up; otherwise the gift is no sacrifice. (*CW*, 11:390)

Without such consciousness of our egoism the hazard is that one approaches the Eucharist "with the unavowed purpose and tacit expectation of purchasing the good will of the Deity," an attitude which turns the Eucharist into a "worthless simulacrum of sacrifice" (*CW*, 11:390).

Understood in this light, the relationship of penance to the Eucharist takes on a new meaning. The confession of sin precedes the Eucharistic celebration in order to make the penitent more "worthy" to participate; not worthy in the sense of a legalistic freedom from sin and guilt, but in the sense of a heightened awareness of sin in the form of that deeply rooted egoism which inspires all our transgressions. In Jung's view, it is precisely our being unconscious of such egoism that constitutes the chief obstacle to the offering of true sacrifice.

NOTES

1. Jolande Jacobi, *The Psychology of C. G. Jung* (London: Routledge and Kegan Paul, 1968), p. 8.
2. *The Collected Works of C. G. Jung*, ed. Gerhard Adler, Michael Fordham, and Herbert Read, 20 vols. (London: Routledge and Kegan Paul, 1953–1979), 8:342. In this chapter all further quotations of Jung's writings are from the *Collected Works* (hereafter referred to as *CW*) and are cited in the text by volume and paragraph numbers.

3.   Frieda Fordham, *An Introduction to Jung's Psychology* (Harmondsworth, Eng.: Penguin, 1966), p. 77.
4.   Erich Fromm, *Sigmund Freud's Mission* (New York: Harper, 1959), pp. 53–54.
5.   Victor White, *God and the Unconscious* (London: Fontana, 1960), p. 77.
6.   Fordham, *An Introduction to Jung's Psychology*, p. 21.
7.   See Paul Tillich, *The Shaking of the Foundations* (New York: Scribner's, 1948), pp. 153–63.
8.   Paul Tillich, *The Courage to Be* (London: Fontana, 1962), p. 160.
9.   Charles Hanna, *The Face of the Deep: The Religious Ideas of C. G. Jung* (Philadelphia: Westminster, 1967), p. 95.

Chapter 5
Faith and Dogma

WE have identified the question asked by the "new style" of natural theology as follows: What quality or aspect of human existence correlates with and makes meaningful those realities of which religion speaks? An examination of Jung's description of the individuation process points to the structural components of the collective unconscious—the archetypes—as that which makes God and religion meaningful for human existence. Religious realities—including God—are, for Jung, symbolic expressions of archetypal themes and in particular of the desire for rebirth or wholeness which characterizes the human psyche. In the preceding chapter we have examined Jung's explanation of the "numinous" quality of religious symbols in terms of their meaningful relationship to the archetypes of the collective unconscious. It is this quality of religious symbols—including the Christian sacramental signs—which accounts, from the psychological perspective, for their power to bring about real change in human personality. They are, to use Jung's phrase, "symbols of transformation" which direct the energy of the psyche towards the psychological and religious goal of wholeness or selfhood.

In Jung's view, religious dogmas have the same kind of symbolic function; they are symbolic expressions of archetypal themes and motifs and, therefore, of our inner unconscious experience. In this respect, they have the same function (of expressing archetypal ideas) as the ancient myths; they are in fact modern substitutes for myths. Since Jung believed that the archetypal structure of the psyche was the human basis of religion, he felt it was important that religious dogmas retain their connection with this inner experience; otherwise, religious belief would lose its human meaning and the transforming and healing power it shares with symbol and myth. "Myths and fairytales," Jung explained, "give expression to unconscious processes, and their retelling causes these processes to come alive again and be recollected, thereby re-establishing the connection between conscious and unconscious."[1]

Unfortunately, as logical, rational discourse and the scientific world view replace mythical and symbolic language, dogma begins increasingly to lose its vital link with the inner experience of the psyche. When this happens, it also loses its symbolic, archetypal meaning and becomes a mere statement about objective reality. "God," for example, is taken to refer to the existence of an objective transcendent reality and loses its symbolic connection with the archetype of wholeness or totality. Dogma thereby begins to lose its connection with the inner life and experience of the believer. It becomes a statement of a truth beyond reason but accepted on faith only, without being rooted in experience. The result, in Jung's words, is that "dogma no longer formulates anything, no longer expresses anything; it has become a tenet to be accepted in and for itself, with no basis in any experience that would demonstrate its truth" (*CW*, 9[2]:276). The further problem is that, once dogma has lost its symbolic meaning and power and has been reduced to a statement about objective reality, it has a difficult time holding its own against scientific truth. It appears to the modern mind as "a language and outlook that have become alien to our present way of thinking" (*CW*, 9[2]:271).

In the light of Jung's symbolic interpretation of dogma, Antonio Moreno has stated: "The God of Jung is inside man and he calls a systematic blindness the prejudice that God is outside man."[2] This statement is probably an inaccurate assessment of Jung's thought since Jung is careful to avoid a simple identification of God with the unconscious or with the God-archetype. What is true, however, is that for Jung religious dogmas and concepts such as the God-image are, from the psychological perspective, projections of archetypal ideas and values, and when the link to these inner experiences and processes is severed the dogma loses its *human* meaning and vitality. It becomes an objective statement to be believed, not a symbol that transforms.

It is necessary, therefore, to withdraw this projection from external reality and reconnect the dogma with the inner psychic reality. It is for this reason that the church cannot confine its teachings to rationalistic doctrinal formulas but must retain the use of mythical and symbolic language, for it is through such language that life transcends the banalities of everyday existence and finds a larger context of meaning. By way of example, Jung refers to the belief of the Pueblo Indians that they are the sons of Father

Sun—a belief which "gives their life a perspective and a goal beyond their individual and limited existence. It leaves ample room for the unfolding of their personality, and is infinitely more satisfying than the certainty that one is and will remain the underdog in a department store." In the same way, St. Paul's conviction that he was not merely "a wandering weaver of carpets" but a messenger of the Lord was a myth which "took possession of him and made him something greater than a mere craftsman," just as the myth of the God-man lifted Jesus "out of the carpenter's shop and the mental narrowness of his surroundings" (*CW*, 18:567–68).

Such myths represent archetypal models for human behaviour, and the living out of the myth gives one's life a meaning beyond personal pleasure or social usefulness. The myth is a symbolic expression of the deepest human need—the need for meaning. For this reason mythical language survives since, as Moreno observes, "contemporary man did not lose yet the power of imitation of archetypal paradigms; nor the desire of transcendence and suprahuman models; nor the longing for unity, for paradise, for salvation; nor the riddles of life, sexuality, evil, suffering, religion and death; nor his desire for integration with the cosmos; nor the horror of history, nor the craving of being beyond time or space; nor the desire for eternity and eternal happiness; nor his attraction for heroes, monsters, fairies, angels, demons, and gods."[3]

Jung complains: "We have stripped all things of their mystery and numinosity; nothing is holy any longer" (*CW*, 18:582). This is particularly true of religious dogmas. When they lose contact with "the numinous psychic powers that forever control man's fate" (*CW*, 18:582), they become logic-defying objects of faith rather than "mysteries" which give life meaning. As a psychologist of religion Jung did not hesitate to go beyond the study of the religious personality and to study the psychological meaning of "religious contents," including dogma. I want to suggest that it is in Jung's analysis of the symbolic, archetypal, experiential meaning of three basic Christian doctrines—God, the Trinity, and the Incarnation—that we may find the fundamentals of a psychologically based natural theology.

God and the God-Image

In Jung's view, as we have seen, the psychological value of religious images consists in the fact that they are conscious symbols of the unconscious quest for wholeness—conscious representations onto which the archetype of the self is projected. Likewise, the various God-images produced by the religious imagination have a similar function; they are conscious symbols representing the archetype of wholeness or totality. For Jung, therefore, God is "psychologically real" since the God-image, as a symbol of totality or wholeness, "is immediately related to, or identical with, the self, and everything that happens to the God-image has an effect on the latter" (*CW*, 9[2]:170). In other words, whatever one might say about God as an ontological reality, the self archetype certainly exists in the human psyche, and this is what is projected onto external reality in our various conscious conceptions and representations of God. For this reason, it may equally be called the "God archetype," though, as we shall see, Jung has reason to prefer the term *self*.

In thus describing the basis of religion and religious belief as a "psychic fact"—the God or self archetype—I believe Jung has reformulated St. Anselm's ontological argument for the existence of God, but in a way which is consistent with our new understanding of natural theology and which therefore avoids the logical fallacies usually associated with the traditional form of this argument. Anselm's starting point had also been a "psychic fact"— the concept of a most perfect being. From the logical existence of this concept he argues for the real existence of a supreme being, for it would be contradictory to think of a most perfect being as not existing. In summary, the argument runs: God is that than which nothing greater can be conceived. But that than which nothing greater can be conceived must exist since, if it existed only in the mind, then a greater being could be thought of, namely, one having real existence. Therefore, God exists.[4]

Paul Tillich, in discussing Anselm's ontological argument, notes that the argument has been accepted by some of history's greatest scholars (Descartes, Leibniz) and flatly rejected by others (Aquinas, Kant). "How is it possible," he asks, "for the greatest thinkers to be divided on this argument?"[5] His answer is based on the distinction between content and form. Those who accept the argument emphasize its content; those who reject it reject its

form and point out that the conclusion is invalid. Tillich believes
that both sides are correct. To reject the form of the argument is
to point out the logical fallacy involved in trying to prove the existence of something outside the mind on the basis of mental concepts.
To accept the content of the argument is to recognize the fact that,
while it fails as an argument to prove the existence of a supreme
being, it nevertheless represents a valid approach to the question
of God, for such an approach "is neither an argument, nor does
it deal with the existence of God."[6] This approach is what Tillich
calls the "ontological method."

We have already discussed in chapter 1 Tillich's distinction
between the cosmological and ontological methods as ways of knowing and experiencing God. It will be recalled that the cosmological
method is an objective approach to the question of God in which
the created universe is seen as providing objective evidence for the
existence of a supreme being who is the author of that universe.
God's existence becomes a logical deduction, the conclusion of a
process of reasoning. In the ontological method, on the other hand,
the approach to the question of God is more subjective; God is
encountered not through a process of reasoning but as a matter
of immediate awareness. God is not the object discovered by the
human subject; he is that which transcends and precedes the distinction between subject and object, the principle of being in which
both subject and object participate. As we have seen, the immediate
awareness of the principle or ground of one's being cannot be turned
into an argument for the existence of a supreme being; hence the
failure of the ontological argument. Tillich's God is the "God
beyond God," the principle of being or being as such which precedes the subject-object split, which is the basis of objective arguments for the existence of a supreme being. The "truth" of the
ontological argument is thus seen in its starting point, which makes
the awareness of God the result of mental contents, a component
of human self-consciousness not dependent on the objective evidence
of the created universe. In Tillich's view, human self-consciousness
carries with it the awareness of our participation in that which is
unconditional or absolute. This awareness is therefore "independent
of any encounter with our world."[7]

If the awareness of God is an accompaniment of human self-
awareness, it becomes self-authenticating, that is, independent of
any scientific, historical, or rational demonstration. As we saw in

chapter 1, this attempt to make faith and the awareness of God self-authenticating and to discover the subjective basis of that awareness was a preoccupation of theological existentialists such as Kierkegaard, Bultmann, and Tillich. In this respect, their work is a reaffirmation of the ontological method—a reaffirmation which, though necessary, carries with it what is to some a disturbing corollary. If religious belief is self-authenticating and independent of our encounter with our world, then it becomes more difficult to think of the world as "God's world," the locus for the discovery of God, the visible evidence of the invisible God. In this sense the world is no longer "sacred" but totally secularized. If the premise of one's theological reflection is that the physical universe gives no evidence of God, that universe then becomes the exclusive domain of science and technology, and there is created the potential (which has now become a grim actuality) for the abuse and pollution of the physical environment thus stripped of its "sacred" character. In his critique of liberation theology, Schubert Ogden describes much of contemporary theology as being in bondage to an exaggerated "homocentrism" in which nature is seen as having value only through human beings; that is, as being without intrinsic value, but having only an instrumental value for the realization of human potentialities.[8] Such a devaluing of nature would not be surprising if the main thrust of Christian apologetics were to make faith "independent of any encounter with our world."

Both these approaches to the question of God leave themselves open, it would seem, to criticism. The cosmological method appears to be excessively objective in that it objectifies a reality which ultimately cannot be objectified, which is not an object existing among others; the ontological method, on the other hand, appears to be excessively subjective since it leaves God insufficiently related to the physical universe. The question, therefore, arises: Is there an approach to the question of God which avoids both these extremes? I believe that Jung's archetypal psychology provides the beginnings of such an approach. As we have seen, the "God beyond God" was for Jung the unconscious God archetype, of which our conscious God-images are symbols. This is the archetype of wholeness or totality, which from the psychological perspective is the archetype of the self.

It is important for a clear understanding of the relationship of God and the self to introduce Jung's distinction between the archetype of the self and the archetypal images of the self. The archetype is not apprehended directly; it is form without content and, therefore, essentially irrepresentable. But as a predisposition to see reality in a certain way it is projected onto the various images of the self in the world of external reality. (Jung mentions "natural" symbols of the self or wholeness, such as mandala and quarternity symbols, as well as religious symbols, such as the cross or the figure of Christ.) The basis of Jung's psychology of religion is the correspondence between, on the one hand, the psychological distinction between the essentially irrepresentable archetype of the self and the archetypal images in which its meaning is approximated in a conscious way, and, on the other hand, the theological distinction between God as essentially unknowable as he is in himself and the images which represent God in human consciousness. The link between God and the self archetype is, in the first instance, that both are essentially unknowable. Aniela Jaffe states: "The unfathomability of God and the unfathomability of the self account for the synonymity, not the identity, of the two concepts."[9]

God and the self are not identical in Jung's thought, but at the level of experience (the aspect of the religious phenomenon that the psychology of religion deals with) they are indistinguishable. Both represent the experience of wholeness or totality. For Jung, the wealth of images, symbols, myths, rituals, and dogmas which make up the history of religions points to the existence of a God archetype which is indistinguishable from the archetype of the self. "Unity and totality," he states, "stand at the highest point on the scale of objective values because their symbols can no longer be distinguished from the *imago Dei*. Hence all statements about the God-image apply also to the empirical symbols of totality" (*CW*, 9[2]:60). This evidence for the existence of an archetype is certainly not a proof for the existence of God of the sort found in traditional natural theology. It does not answer the question "Is there a God?" as Jung himself insists: "This is certainly not to say that what we call the unconscious is identical with God or is set up in his place. It is simply the medium from which religious experience seems to flow. As to what the further cause of such experience may be, the answer to this lies beyond the range of human knowledge. Knowledge of God is a transcendental problem" (*CW*, 10:565). As a psychologist Jung is content to deal with the less ultimate question "Why is man religious?" I believe that it is in Jung's answer to this latter question, an answer which avoids both the extreme objectivity of the cosmological method and the extreme subjectivity of the ontological method, that we can perhaps find a restatement of the ontological argument which avoids the logical fallacies of the original.

Jung would be in complete agreement with the objection raised against the cosmological method and all forms of supranaturalism, that they objectify a reality which cannot be objectified. His psychological approach to the question of God can loosely be described as ontological in the sense that God is to be discovered "within" and not in the world of external reality. In the words of Paul Stern, the God whom many people could no longer discover in their world or even in the church was rediscovered by Jung "literally underground . . . in the catacombs of the psyche known as the region of the unconscious."[10] What, for Jung, is psychologically real is the archetype of totality, which exists in the human psyche and which is projected onto various external conceptions and representations of God. But the reality of the archetype is unconscious; we become conscious of it only by encountering the images and symbols which are projected onto external reality or come into consciousness through dreams and phantasies. Jung's complaint is that we mistake the image for the reality and, therefore, think of God as a supreme being existing as an object over against humanity. The result is that dogmatic formulations become statements about this objective reality unrelated to our inner experience (*CW*, 9[2]:276).

At the same time, Jung's insistence that God is discovered within the psyche seems to avoid the extreme subjectivity of the ontological method. He insists that what is discovered within the psyche is not necessarily "subjective" or of our own making since the collective unconscious is a transpersonal, objective reality. The God archetype, therefore, as a component of this "objective psyche," has an existence of its own independent of individual consciousness. The God archetype, then, is an "objective" reality but exists "within." This means, on the one hand, that its reality cannot be "proved" in a scientific way but only experienced since science deals with external realities. "Science," Jung argues, "has never discovered any 'God,' epistemological criticism proves the impossibility of knowing God, but the psyche comes forward with the assertion of the experience of God. God is a psychic fact of immediate experience, otherwise there would never have been any talk of God" (*CW*, 8:625).

On the other hand it means that, since the God "within" is an unconscious reality, he can only be experienced through our encounters with projections of that reality in the world of external reality, the various manifestations of the God-image. Thus the physical universe is not devalued or desacralized. Jung is not as willing as Schleiermacher to renounce any religious claims on the physical universe and to look upon nature as the exclusive realm of science and technology. Though God is "within," the external world is still "God's world" because of its symbolic function. External reality gives evidence of God, not because it proves the objective existence of a supreme being, but because it is only in the world of external reality that we encounter this inner reality since the unconscious archetype must be projected onto external symbols in order to become conscious. Indeed, Jung argues, it is important to project this unconscious archetype onto some conscious God-image; otherwise the archetype of wholeness or totality—"the highest point on the scale of objective values"—will be projected onto some less worthy object: "There is in the psyche some superior power, and if it is not consciously a god, it is the 'belly,' at least in St. Paul's words. I therefore consider it wiser to acknowledge the idea of God consciously; for, if we do not, something else is made God, usually something quite inappropriate and stupid such as only an 'enlightened' intellect would hatch forth" (*CW*, 7:110). Thus, while the God archetype is an inner reality, the world of dreams, phantasies, myth, symbol, ritual, and dogma provides a wealth of what Jung insists on calling "empirical evidence" of that reality.

The question, however, remains: What significance does such evidence have for the "question of God" in view of the fact that it demonstrates, if anything, only the validity of a "psychic fact" (the God or self archetype)? Jung carefully avoids inferring from the existence of this *typos* or imprint in the psyche the existence of an "imprinter": "The religious point of view, understandably enough, puts the accent on the imprinter, whereas scientific psychology emphasizes the *typos*, the imprint—the only thing it can understand" (*CW*, 12:20). To preserve the "archetypal indefiniteness" of this psychic fact, and to avoid linking it exclusively with any of the particular God-images found in the history of religions, Jung prefers the term *self* to describe the archetype corresponding to such images. At the same time, he maintains that the self cannot be distinguished from the God-image "except by incontestable and unprovable faith" (*CW*, 13:289). In other words, as we have already seen, Jung does not deal with the question "Does God exist?" but with what is the more appropriate question for the psychology of religion, "Why is man religious?" "The idea of God," he states, "is an absolutely necessary psychological function of an irrational nature, which has nothing whatever to do with the question of God's existence. The human intellect can never answer this question, still less give any proof of God. Moreover, such proof is superfluous, for the idea of an all powerful divine Being is present everywhere, unconsciously if not consciously, because it is an archetype" (*CW*, 7:110).

Psychology can only discover the archetype—the human basis of religion—and cannot deal with the more ultimate question of God's objective existence. But if this limitation is appropriate for the psychology of religion (as for all the "sciences of religion"), it is being increasingly recognized (as we saw in chapter 1) that the same limitation is to be imposed on natural theology, which originally produced "proofs" for the existence of God. Carl Braaten argues that "the Christian doctrine of God stands or falls with God's self-identification in Jesus of Nazareth."[11] In other words, the ultimate source of belief, on the human side, is what Jung calls "incontestable and unprovable faith." Implied in Braaten's statement is the recognition that traditional natural theology is "no longer giving us knowledge of who and what God is—or even if he exists for sure."[12] The new style of natural theology which Braaten and others call for would concern itself, not with speculation about the existence and nature of God, but with locating the area of human experience which gives rise to the question of God. "Natural theology," he suggests, "cannot tell us who and what God is, but it can trace out the contexts and conditions in human existence and in the world which correlate to the meaning of the word 'God' when it is used."[13]

I am suggesting that this is precisely what Jung has done in arguing for the existence of a structural component of the human psyche (the self archetype) which correlates with the word "God." In doing so he has restated, I believe, the ontological argument while observing its limitations. Anselm had argued from the existence of a "psychic fact" (the concept of a most perfect being) to the existence of an objective, transcendent reality, an argument whose logical fallacies have been pointed out by all its critics from Aquinas to Tillich. Jung, on the other hand, argues from the exist-ence of a psychic fact (the self or God archetype) to the fact of man's natural religiousness or his desire for self-transcendence, which in this instance takes the form of the quest for wholeness. This form of the ontological argument has meaning for a natural theology which seeks to demonstrate not the existence of God but what Braaten calls "the fundamental humanness of the question of God."[14] For Jung, the God archetype is a psychic fact whose existence requires no logical demonstration. At the same time it cannot be used to prove the existence of God as a supreme being having external, objective existence. This double affirmation accounts for Jung's contention that while the ontological argument in its classical form is "neither argument nor proof" (*CW*, 6:61), nevertheless "the *consensus gentium* proves that in the statement 'God is, because he is thought,' Anselm was right" (*CW*, 6:62).

The Trinity

In Jung's psychological interpretation, dogmas have a symbolic function and put the believer in touch with archetypal contents of the unconscious. When stripped of this symbolic function, they lose their connections with our inner, unconscious experience and become, as we have seen, mere statements about objective realities to be believed on faith. This is particularly true of the doctrine of the Trinity, which for most contemporary Christians has become an object of faith with little connection with their own human expe-rience. In his essay "A Psychological Approach to the Dogma of the Trinity," Jung remarks: "The Trinity and its inner life process appears as a closed circle, a self-contained divine drama in which man plays, at most, a passive part." Consequently it is "difficult to see what the Trinity could possibly mean for us, either prac-tically, morally, or symbolically" (*CW*, 11:226). A dogma thus stripped of its symbolic meaning is unable to play a part in the integration of personality since it no longer confronts the believer with the archetypal contents of his own unconscious. Jung complains that theology, by ignoring this human, archetypal meaning of dogma, "proclaims doctrines which nobody understands, and demands a faith which nobody can manufacture" (*CW*, 11:285).

A further consequence of the loss of symbolic meaning is that doctrines like the Trinity tend to lose any significance within the Christian system of belief. The concept of a triune God seems to introduce an unnecessary complexity into one's belief in one God. In reality, however, if, as Jung suggests, the human psyche consciously or unconsciously perceives God as a symbol of totality, then the doctrine of the Trinity addresses itself to the problems associated with belief in one God. The human person, in order to experience personal wholeness, must go beyond himself to form bonds of relatedness with others. Absolute autonomy is beyond our capacities, and the attempt to achieve it ends in the experience of isolation and alienation. It has always been difficult, therefore, from the human point of view to appreciate the autonomy and self-sufficiency of a God who lives in such "splendid isolation," who completely transcends and has no need of his creation. The Trinity, however, reveals that God, being a trinity of persons, has within himself the relatedness and the exchange of knowledge and love which the human person must go outside of himself to find. The doctrine of the Trinity asserts that only God can be absolutely autonomous and therefore a symbol of totality or completeness.

It is within the context of this inability of the conscious mind to reconcile oneness with wholeness that we must situate Jung's reflections on the Trinity. Symbols such as the Trinity are the means by which the conscious mind encounters the archetype of the self or of personal wholeness since "the conscious mind can form absolutely no conception of this totality, because it includes not only the conscious but also the unconscious psyche, which is, as such, inconceivable and irrepresentable" (*CW*, 11:230). Therefore it must be represented to consciousness in a symbolic way. The Trinity is one of these symbols, and Jung sees in it a twofold symbolism, or "expression of the psyche." First, the Trinity is a symbolic expression of the "process of unconscious maturation taking place within the individual" (*CW*, 11:287). As a symbol of the self it represents the whole process of individuation, the three persons representing the three stages of personality growth: original, unconscious unity; conscious differentiation and polarity; higher unity (union of conscious and unconscious). Secondly, the Trinity "denotes a process of conscious realization continuing over the centuries" (*CW*, 11:288). This refers to the process of humanity's

growth in consciousness, which parallels the progressive development of the image of God in human consciousness. In Jung's
words, "God becomes manifest in the human act of reflection"
(*CW*, 11:238).

It is in the light of the Trinity as a symbol of the process
involved in both human maturation (individuation) and the development of the God-image that Jung interprets the meaning of the
three Persons. The Father represents God as one and indivisible
and, therefore, the first stage of human growth, which is characterized by an original unconscious unity. This first stage of growth
is one of non-differentiation and unself-consciousness—the childhood state of identification with parental figures. This corresponds
to primitive conceptions of the deity in which God is both good
and evil and unconscious of the differentiation. In "Answer to Job"
Jung describes the character of the God with whom Job has to con-
tend in this way. Yahweh is "too unconscious to be moral. Morality
presupposes consciousness . . . . He is everything in its totality;
therefore, among other things, he is total justice and also its total
opposite" (*CW*, 11:574). Yahweh is autocratic and punitive towards
Job, and his behaviour "is the behaviour of an unconscious being
who cannot be judged morally. Yahweh is a *phenomenon* and as Job
says 'not a man' " (*CW*, 11:600). This state is representative of
childhood consciousness, which has not yet consciously differentiated
between good and evil. "The father," Jung states, "denotes the
earlier stage of consciousness when one was still a child, still dependent on a definite, ready-made pattern of existence which is habitual
and has the character of law. It is a passive, unreflecting condition,
a mere awareness of what is given, without intellectual or moral
judgment" (*CW*, 11:270).

The Son represents the second stage of growth and of the
development of the God-image. In terms of personal development,
the growth of consciousness and self-awareness means that conscious
choice and decision replace habit. As the adolescent differentiates
himself from his parents and develops his individuality, he makes
conscious differentiations between self and others, masculine and
feminine, good and evil. As we have seen, the individual's identification with one pole of these dichotomies leads to a one-sided development, since aspects of his total personality which are incompatible
with his conscious identity are relegated to the dark, unadapted,
unconscious side of personality. The result is a sense of dissatis-

faction, incompleteness, alienation from the self—a sense of something missing. This stage of growth corresponds to conceptions and images of God in which masculine and feminine, good and evil, are differentiated.

The differentiation of the masculine and feminine aspects of the deity (both being necessary for completeness) appears in ancient mythology in the images of the "syzygy" or divine pair, such as Adonis and Aphrodite or Osiris and Isis. In the Judaeo-Christian tradition Jung points to the appearance of Sophia, the Old Testament embodiment of Wisdom. Sophia represents for Jung the "feminine" side of God, without which God is incomplete, and that aspect of himself about which God remains unconscious in his autocratic treatment of Job. Nevertheless, it is to this side of God that Job looks for compassion against Yahweh's punitive measures, for Sophia "reveals herself to men as a friendly helper and advocate against Yahweh, and shows them the bright side, the kind, just, and amiable aspect of their God" (CW, 11:623). Jung's contention is that the introduction of this feminine symbol makes the God-image a more adequate symbol of totality since the one-sidedly masculine God represents the ideal of perfection rather than completeness. "Perfection is a masculine desideratum," he says, "while woman inclines by nature to *completeness*" (CW, 11:620). Completeness is the necessary counterpart to perfection for "just as completeness is always imperfect, so perfection is always incomplete" (CW, 11:620).

The controversial character of Jung's "Answer to Job" rests on the perception of Job as morally superior to Yahweh in that he appeals for his vindication to this compassionate side of God, of which God himself is unconscious. Job is more aware of God's goodness and justice than God is. Moreover, in Jung's interpretation, the traditional doctrine of the atonement is reversed for the Incarnation is perceived as God's "answer to Job"; that is, God becomes man to atone for *God's* crime against Job, thus making up for his previous lack of self-awareness.[15] This Incarnation becomes a continuing process through the sending of the Holy Spirit, whose task is to create a new humanity in the image of God, characterized now by completeness rather than perfection. As with the Sophia imagery, this completeness or wholeness is symbolized in Christian tradition by feminine symbols—in the vision of St. John (Rev. 12:1-3) by the woman "adorned with the sun" and her offspring and, in our own times, Jung believed, by the doctrine of the assumption of Mary, who—"as the bride of God and Queen of Heaven—holds the place of the Old Testament Sophia" (CW, 11:625). The definition of this dogma, which Jung considered "the most important religious event since the Reformation" (CW, 11:752), symbolically restores the feminine principle to the deity for "Mary as the bride is united with the Son in the heavenly bridal-chamber, and, as Sophia, with the Godhead" (CW, 11:743).

As representative of the feminine principle, Mary's symbolic function is to supply what is missing in the God-image and thus transform that image into a symbol of completeness rather than mere perfection. This symbolic function is diminished somewhat, Jung believes, by the doctrinal exaltation of Mary as immaculately conceived, her sinlessness and perpetual virginity raising her to the status of a goddess. In addition to making the Incarnation incomplete, since Mary is thereby perceived as not fully human, this exalting of Mary is "injurious to the feminine principle of imperfection or completeness" because it makes Mary to some extent a symbol of perfection like Christ, and "the more the feminine ideal is bent in the direction of the masculine, the more the woman loses her power to compensate the masculine striving for perfection" (CW, 11:627). Church teaching, of course, does not deify Mary, who is still a creature in spite of her exalted position. Nevertheless the encouraging of veneration of Mary by the church, both by doctrinal definitions and pastoral practice, was in response, Jung believed, to a "popular movement and the psychological need behind it" (CW, 11:748). This popular movement was the need experienced by the faithful for an intercessor and mediatrix who would take her place alongside the Trinity; the psychological need refers to "tremendous archetypal happenings in the psyche of the individual and the masses" (CW, 11:749).

To understand this archetypal happening we must recall Jung's words about the indistinguishability of the self and God archetypes. From the psychological perspective, it is the self archetype which is projected onto the various God-images, including the Christian symbol of the Trinity, thus making them meaningful for human existence as symbols of wholeness. On the basis of his clinical experience, however, Jung proposes that from the human and archetypal points of view there is something missing in the Christian symbol of the Trinity, since the natural symbols of the self which appear both in mythology and in the dreams of his patients appear as mandala and quaternity or fourfold symbols. The human psyche, therefore, tends to transform the threefold Trinitarian symbol into a quaternity (this being the natural fourfold symbol representing the four elements of creation or the four functions of the psyche and therefore wholeness). The resulting quaternity symbol represents the Trinity plus a fourth element, and that element is an earthy, bodily, feminine element (*CW*, 11:107).

In the person of Christ, however, this quaternity archetype in the unconscious becomes for the believer an objective reality. In the person of Christ, the "Son of Man," "born of a woman," this earthly, physical element is added to the Trinity to form a quaternity, so that Christ becomes a symbol of wholeness or selfhood. In his appendix to Victor White's *God and the Unconscious*, Gebhard Frei sees Christ as the mediator between God and humanity, God and his kingdom, and thus a symbol of the wholeness that is achieved through the union of the human and the divine:

> Above is the Trinity, the lightsome male principle, below is Matter, Woman; the Kingdom between them is the Mediator, the Son, the Intercessor. Completion or fulfilment exists only when the fourth principle is brought into the Trinity; thus Mary is assumed into heaven even in her material form, bodily. The King of Heaven and the Queen of Heaven unite themselves through the act of their Son. The fourth principle is the principle of the Mother: "Mother Mary" and "Mother Church," the Kingdom. Christ is the Mediator who links God with his Kingdom. He is himself the divine Bridegroom, and his Kingdom, the Church, is the Bride, and their full *coniunctio* is the end or *dénouement* of the whole process. Matter has not been eliminated or excluded, on the contrary, "there will be a new heaven and a new earth": spiritualised matter and embodied spirit: *wholeness*.[16]

Though Jung agrees that Christ exemplifies the archetype of the self, he also sees the figure of Christ as lacking something which is necessary in order to be a symbol of wholeness, namely, the "dark side" of human personality—the primitive, earthy, animal side, including the human propensity for evil. This dark side of the psyche also represents the missing fourth element in the Trinity. As we have seen, it is an element which must be included in the concept of wholeness and, in Jung's view, in all symbols of totality, including the God-image. Hence, in "Answer to Job," Yahweh is described as having this dark, unconscious side. It is precisely this element, however, which Jung sees as being dogmatically excluded from the sinless personality of Christ and projected onto another symbol, that of Satan or Antichrist. The Christ-Antichrist polarity corresponds to the clash of spiritual and earthly elements in the Christian personality. It is with the coming of Christ that these opposites become manifest and objectified.

The Incarnation, therefore, represents a further differentiation of Yahweh's consciousness or of the God-image. As the Sophia/Mary symbolism differentiates the masculine and feminine aspects of the Godhead, so the Christ/Antichrist symbolism differentiates the good and evil, light and dark, aspects of that same totality. The Antichrist, Jung argues, is the inevitable shadow cast by Christ, who incarnates only the light side of God. In Christian teaching God is identified with this light aspect (Christ) and becomes the good and loving father. By way of compensation, Satan appears as the incarnation of the "dark side" of God. Again the human psyche has turned the Trinity into a quaternity, and therefore a symbol of the self, by introducing a fourth element (Antichrist) onto which the dark side of personality is projected.

Whatever one's position might be regarding the theological implications of such a theory,[17] it is difficult to disagree with Jung's contention that the ideal of wholeness must include some kind of assimilation of, or coming to terms with, the dark side of personality. If the Trinity symbolizes the process of individuation in the various stages, then it should reflect, in Jung's view, the conflict engendered by the conscious differentiations associated with the growth of consciousness, including the differentiation of good and evil. For Jung, the Incarnation represents the conflict of good and evil in God, and those in whom the image of God is realized must undergo the same conflict. This conflict is symbolized by the Cross—another quaternity symbol.

We have seen that the third and final stage of the individuation process refers to a higher state of consciousness achieved through a union of those opposites which come into opposition through the growth of consciousness—a *coniunctio oppositorum*. In "Answer to Job" this third stage is represented by the coming of the Holy Spirit, whose function is to continue the Incarnation in "empirical man" thus creating a new humanity characterized by completeness rather than perfection. In the Trinity symbolism the Spirit represents the third element common to the Father and Son, who puts an end to the duality caused by the conflict between the Son and the shadow he casts (Satan) and restores the lost unity but at a higher level. In the same way, in the context of the individuation process, the reconciling symbol brings about a union of the opposites created by the growth of consciousness and leads to a higher state of consciousness.

In Jung's psychological interpretation of the Trinity as, in actuality, a quaternity symbol of the self, the original unity of the Father is an unconscious unity of good and evil. Christ and the devil, as incarnations of the "light" and "dark" sides of the Father, represent the differentiation and conflict of good and evil. The Spirit, as the life common to the Father and Son, is the reconciling principle which resolves this conflict. "Looked at from a quaternity standpoint, the Holy Ghost is a reconciliation of opposites and hence the answer to the suffering in the Godhead which Christ personifies" (*CW*, 11:260). As we have seen, the suffering to which he refers is symbolic of the conflict which, according to Jung, humanity must endure until a time when our conceptions of good and evil are sufficiently relativized that a morality "beyond good and evil" becomes possible (*CW*, 11:258). Translated in terms of the moral life of the Christian, this means that conscious legalistic differentiations between good and evil lose their ultimacy as norms for moral decision-making. The ultimate moral norm which relativizes the letter of the law is "the Spirit"—that same Spirit which Jung sees as continuing the Incarnation in "empirical man" of that God who combines both good and evil, that is, who is beyond our conscious conceptions of good and evil. Thus the goal of such moral decision-making is completeness rather than perfection. Charles Hanna describes the effect of this continuing Incarnation:

> The tension between good and evil is held in a new synthesis and understanding. In it we will be more able to see the evil that clings to all our good and the good that can even come through what appears to be

evil. We are saved from being torn asunder by this paradox through the Holy Spirit who delivers us from a legalistic black and white conception of good and evil and in whom we are able to ascertain what is the will of God in any particular circumstance.[18]

Incarnation and Redemption

Thus far we have seen that Jung's answer to the question of natural theology points to the archetype of the self—a structural component of the unconscious psyche—as that which gives human meaning to the concept of God. In this context God-images in general are symbolic of selfhood or totality, and the image of the Trinity is symbolic of the stages of the individuation process by which the ideal of wholeness is approximated. If we turn our attention now to the central Christian doctrine of the Incarnation and redemption, and to a possible psychological interpretation of that doctrine within the context of Jungian theory, two points, I believe, will become evident: (1) Symbolic meaning is here attached not simply to a concept or image but to an historical person and event. (2) Incarnation and redemption must be seen together as aspects of the same symbol for, from the symbolic point of view, Christ does not become a complete symbol of the self apart from his redemptive death and resurrection.

The most obvious sense in which Christ is a symbol of the self consists in the dogmatic assertion that he is God incarnate—the man in whom God becomes human. As such, he is symbolic of that continuing Incarnation in "empirical man" which is the work of the Holy Spirit. The Jungian view would maintain that, from the psychological point of view, since the self and God archetypes are indistinguishable, this Incarnation refers to the assimilation of the self archetype into our conscious attitudes; that is, the achieving of wholeness through the process of individuation. "This metaphysical process," Jung says, "is known to the psychology of the unconscious as the individuation process" (*CW*, 11:755). The achieving of selfhood, however, involves confronting and coming to terms with the "shadow" or dark, unadapted side of personality. For this reason, as we have seen, Jung sees the figure of Christ as an incomplete symbol of the self since it lacks this dark aspect. To make the symbol complete the psyche projects this dark side onto Christ's opposite—Satan or Antichrist. Though Christ is "our nearest analogy of the self and its meaning," nevertheless, from the psychological perspective, Jung argues, "he corresponds to only one half of the archetype. The other half appears in the Antichrist. The latter is just as much a manifestation of the self, except that he consists of its dark aspect" (*CW*, 9[2]:79). This dark aspect of personality has to be reintegrated in some way into the figure of Christ if it is to serve as a complete symbol of the self: "Psychologically the case is clear, since the dogmatic figure of Christ is so sublime and spotless that everything else turns dark beside it. It is, in fact, so one-sidedly perfect that it demands a psychic complement to restore the balance . . . . The coming of the Antichrist is not just a prophetic prediction—it is an inexorable psychological law" (*CW*, 9[2]:77).

On this point Jung was in conflict with the philosophical and theological tradition which holds that evil is not a positive component of wholeness but merely a *privatio boni*—a negative absence of good. In the light of this doctrine wholeness could be attributed to the sinless figure of Christ since to lack evil was to lack no positive ingredient of wholeness. For Jung, however, evil was the opposite and necessary complement of good. This issue has always been a bone of contention between Jungian and Christian thought, and it is beyond the scope of our discussion to enter into it. It may be helpful, however, to recall that when Jung attributes a dark or evil side to God or Christ, he can only be referring to our human conceptions of good and evil. God is the totality who lies beyond the conflict of good and evil in this sense and in whom the conflict is reconciled. This is reflected in the religious conviction that good can somehow come out of evil circumstances and in the Christian moral conviction that "the good" is not simply identified with the content of legal and moral prescriptions.

It may be, as H. R. Philp has suggested,[19] that the dogmatic view of Christ as a sinless figure demands a psychic complement only because of our narrow conceptions of good and evil, sin and virtue. It was Christ himself who condemned such narrowness and insisted on a virtue which goes deeper "than that of the scribes and Pharisees" (Matt. 5:20). In Jungian terms this means that one's moral striving must aim at wholeness or completeness rather than mere moral perfection. This ideal demands the integration, in some way, of the dark side of personality. Thus, if the figure of Christ is perceived as "sinless" in the sense of reflecting only moral perfection, then it becomes an incomplete symbol of the self—a symbol of perfection rather than wholeness. Since wholeness, however, represents a resolution of the conflict between good and evil—a union of opposites—through the agency of the reconciling symbol, then the complete Christian symbol would not merely be the figure of the sinless Christ but the Christ who is crucified and risen from the dead and whose death and rebirth is therefore a symbol of the "death" of consciousness through this tension of opposites and its rebirth through reimmersion in the unconscious. The crucifixion of Christ represents the crucifixion of the ego seeking completeness—of the ego torn between perfection and completeness. It is this ego which needs redemption, that is, acceptance in spite of its lack of perfection. Such a redemption constitutes a rebirth of self in which completeness replaces perfection and which is symbolized by the death and resurrection of Christ. All who would achieve selfhood must undergo this crucifixion of the ego. "The whole world is God's suffering," Jung maintains, "and every individual man who wants to get anywhere near his own wholeness knows that this is the way of the cross" (*CW*, 11:265).

In this context Christ is for the Christian believer a unique symbol of the self precisely because he is a real historical figure. As Victor White points out, the mythological theme of the dying and rising god, which represents a mythologizing of history and nature, is, in Christ, an historical event: "All this reverses the normal process of faith-memory which, we know, tends to mythologize history; now it is rather the mythological pattern that is realized in historical fact . . . . The inner reality which the ancient rituals had expressed is now lived through."[20] But the original mythological theme of death and rebirth, which the Christ event makes historical, was the projection of an archetypal theme in the human psyche—a symbol related to and giving expression to the archetype of the self. Thus it is not just a myth but the archetypal theme of selfhood which the Christ event actualizes. Seen in this light—as the historical expression of an inner human experience—the figure of Jesus, who in theological language is the incarnate son of God, becomes, psychologically, the incarnation of the archetypal theme of rebirth to wholeness existing in the collective unconscious of humanity. Thus he is not only the fulfillment of the written prophecies of the Old Testament, but, for the person of faith, the fulfillment of the deepest human aspirations.

Such an interpretation does not "psychologize" the mystery of redemption or compromise its theological meaning. On the contrary, it explains the psychological condition of human existence which makes that mystery humanly meaningful (again, the question of natural theology). In Jung's words, recognition of this archetypal theme in the Christ event "forcibly creates the psychological preconditions without which 'redemption' would appear meaningless" (*CW*, 9[2]:125). The Christ figure, he explains, is assimilated into a "psychic matrix" (the archetype) which gives it a universal human meaning: "Had there not been an affinity—magnet!—between the figure of the Redeemer and certain contents of the unconscious, the human mind would never have been able to perceive the light shining in Christ and seize upon it so passionately. The connecting link here is the archetype of the God-man, which on the one hand became historical reality in Christ, and on the other, being eternally present, reigns over the soul in the form of a supraordinate totality, the self" (*CW*, 9[2]:283).

We may further note that the figure of Christ thus understood, namely, as representing the "crucifixion of the ego" torn between completeness and perfection and experiencing a rebirth or resurrection, is a symbol of that kind of transformation of personality which we discussed in chapter 3 as issuing from the experience of grace and faith—the transformation from self-justifying to self-transcending motivation. This crucifixion of the ego is analogous to the inner conflict and frustration experienced by the person who seeks self-justification through the pursuit of that "perfection" represented by legal, ethical, and religious observance. The figure of the sinless Christ is a symbol of the type of Christian life which consists in the pursuit of self-justifying moral and religious perfection and which, as we have seen, is the preliminary phase or preamble to genuine faith existence. Faith becomes possible at the dead end of that pursuit. For Jung, the sinless figure of Christ must be reunited with its opposite—the Antichrist or dark side of personality. It is the "perfect" Christ who must die and be reborn. In the same way, in the faith experience of the believer, the anxiety-producing (crucifying) pursuit of moral and religious perfection must give way to genuine faith, that radical act of trust in God's acceptance of the ego which inevitably fails to achieve the required perfection. It is precisely this failure which leads the believer to acknowledge his lack of rectitude or self-sufficiency; to acknowledge

what the New Testament calls sin and what Jung calls the shadow
or dark side of personality.

This kind of anxiety-producing self-knowledge is what
St. Paul experienced in his pursuit of the perfection demanded by
the Law, as it is experienced by everyone who pursues a moral,
ethical, or religious ideal of perfection. It is the conscious recognition of the futility of this pursuit of self-justifying perfection which
makes faith possible, and therefore the transformation from self-
justifying to self-transcending motives. In the context of Jung's view
of human growth, one would describe this dynamic of faith as the
transcending of ego-consciousness and its self-justifying projections
through the recognition and acceptance of the shadow; that is,
through the recognition of the evil within oneself. Thereby one
moves in the direction of wholeness through the sacrifice of one's
morally righteous, artificial persona and the acceptance of the dark
and previously unrecognized and unaccepted part of one's total self.

Just as faith begins with repentance for the sin which is
revealed in one's striving for moral perfection, genuine growth
towards selfhood begins, in Jung's view, with the recognition of
the shadow. It is only when an individual recognizes and accepts
this proclivity to evil within himself that he is able to withdraw those
projections by which he attributes all evil to others and to forces
outside himself. In this way, as we have seen, human relationships
become possible since each individual realizes that the evil he sees
in others is also in himself, and he is thereby relieved of the necessity
of justifying himself before others or protecting himself from them.
The facade of moral superiority is discarded, and the resulting state
of self-knowledge and humility, which involves the recognition of
imperfection and dependence, is seen by Jung as the basis of human
relationships (*CW*, 10:579). The same dynamic obtains in the faith
experience. The acknowledgement of sinfulness, of the inability
to justify himself, relieves the believer of the necessity of self-
justification and makes it possible for him to enter into the personal
relationship of faith, which is offered to him as a gift or grace. If
the person of faith achieves wholeness or selfhood, it is because
he finds, in the message of God's unconditional acceptance and
forgiveness, the courage to accept and integrate the "dark side"
of his own personality. It is this self-acceptance—the acceptance
of one's *total* self in the light of God's acceptance of that self—
which creates the possibility of self-transcendence by liberating one

from the self-preoccupation implied in the pursuit of moral and religious perfection. We shall return to the moral implications of this experience in a later chapter.

NOTES

1. *The Collected Works of C. G. Jung*, ed. Gerhard Adler, Michael Fordham, and Herbert Read, 20 vols. (London: Routledge and Kegan Paul, 1953–1979), 9(2):280. In this chapter all further quotations of Jung's writings are from the *Collected Works* (hereafter referred to as *CW*) and are cited in the text by volume and paragraph numbers.

2. Antonio Moreno, *Jung, Gods and Modern Man* (Notre Dame, Ind.: University of Notre Dame Press, 1970), p. 83.

3. Ibid., pp. 172–73.

4. *Proslogion*, 1–4.

5. Paul Tillich, *A History of Christian Thought* (London: SCM Press, 1968), p. 164.

6. Paul Tillich, *Theology of Culture* (New York: Oxford University Press, 1964), p. 15.

7. Tillich, *A History of Christian Thought*, p. 165.

8. Schubert Ogden, *Faith and Freedom: Toward a Theology of Liberation* (Nashville: Abingdon Press, 1979), pp. 102–14.

9. Aniela Jaffe, *The Myth of Meaning*, trans. R.F.C. Hull (New York: Penguin, 1975), p. 113.

10. Paul Stern, *C. G. Jung: The Haunted Prophet* (New York: George Braziller, 1976), p. 253.

11. Carl Braaten, *The Future of God* (New York: Harper and Row, 1969), p. 65.

12. Ibid., p. 63.

13. Ibid., p. 64.

14. Ibid.

15. This may be an instance where Jung draws a metaphysical conclusion from psychological data. Though Jung protests that he remains neutral about metaphysical questions, it is not always clear from his mode of expression that he is talking about the God-image in the human psyche and not about God as he is in himself.

16. Victor White, *God and the Unconscious* (London: Fontana, 1960), pp. 261–62.

17. The notion of the "dark side" of God, which may be repugnant to the theologian, is, in Jung's view, psychologically necessary if God is to be a complete symbol of totality. It is helpful to recall that the psychological notion of the God-image as symbolic of that totality which unites opposites is consistent with dialectical theol-

ogy's understanding of God as the mystery in which those things, which to the human mind are opposites, are reconciled.

18.   Charles Hanna, *The Face of the Deep: The Religious Ideas of C. G. Jung* (Philadelphia: Westminster, 1967), pp. 78–79.

19.   H. R. Philp, *Jung and the Problem of Evil* (London: Rockliff, 1958).

20.   White, *God and the Unconscious*, p. 239.

FREUD OR JUNG?

The primal father was the original image of God, the model on which later generations have shaped the figure of God.

Sigmund Freud, *The Future of an Illusion*

Faith is certainly right when it impresses on man's mind and heart how infinitely far away and inaccessible God is; but it also teaches his nearness, his immediate presence, and it is just this nearness which has to be empirically real if it is not to lose all significance. Only that which acts upon me do I recognize as real and actual. But that which has no effect upon me might as well not exist.

Carl Jung, *Answer to Job*

Chapter 6
The Problem of God

IN trying to construct a psychologically based natural theology we have formulated the question of natural theology as follows: What are the psychological roots of belief in a transcendent God? What can we point to in the structure and dynamics of human personality which correlates with the concept of God and makes it meaningful for human existence? To ask this question in the light of the psychological theories of Freud and Jung is to use those theories as interpretive tools to investigate the human meaning of religious and theological concepts in the light of what each theory reveals about the meaning and goals of human existence. In the context of this study the question arises: Which theory is the more adequate tool for interpreting the human meaning of Christianity? At first glance it would appear that, as interpretive tools, the two theories are incompatible. For Jung, as we have seen, religion "properly" understood is conducive to human growth and maturity since the symbolic character of religion correlates with the archetypal structure of the human psyche. Freud, on the other hand, saw religion as a neurotic and regressive father fixation and, therefore, as an impediment to full human development.

This popular view of the two theorists is not, however, without dissenters. We have seen that Erich Fromm accused Jung of reductionism and saw in Freudian theory an attempt to preserve the "ethical core" of religion. In a much more polemical attack, Edward Glover argued that the popularity of Jung's views among the clergy was to be interpreted as a reaction to Freud's negative view of religion and not as a tribute to any alleged religious quality of Jung's theory. "It is all the more necessary therefore," he wrote, "to point out what is apparently effectively concealed in a mass of Jungian verbiage, that so far from being religious in tendency, Jung's system is fundamentally irreligious. Nobody is to care whether God exists, Jung least of all. All that is necessary is to 'experience' an 'attitude' because it 'helps one to live.' "[1] I want to suggest that, as interpretive tools, the two theories are complementary. In answering the question about the psychological roots of religion, Freud emphasizes the experience of and relationship to one's father, while Jung points to the archetype of the self as that which makes God and religion humanly meaningful. These are the psychic contents—the father-image and the self archetype— which are projected, and the resulting God-images correspond to two different ways of understanding God and religion. In order to pursue this comparison, it is necessary to briefly review Freud's analysis of the formation of the God-image as we have already done with Jung. Freud's psychology of religion reveals two major themes: religion as both an illusion and an obsessional neurosis represents a victory for the death instinct; and God is a father figure or substitute father.

I have argued in chapters 2 and 3 that the Christian message of life triumphing over death correlates with the Freudian understanding of the conflict between Eros (life) and death which characterizes human existence, and that the transformation of motives achieved in the faith experience makes agape (the Christian moral ideal) and therefore Eros possible. It should be noted that the New Testament abounds in references to human existence as characterized by the duality of life and death, and to the faith experience of the Christian as passing from death to life. While the "life" in question may be seen as eschatological, as a future inheritance, it is also a present reality and becomes so through the faith and love of the believer. Jesus is the one who "gives life to whom he will" (John 5:21); who has come that humanity "may have life, and have it abundantly" (John 10:10). Jesus describes the person of faith as one who has passed "from death to life" (John 5:24) and himself as the "bread of life" (John 6:48). Again, in the parable of the last judgement (Matt. 25), life is promised to those who practise the works of love (feeding the hungry, etc.) which flow from faith and, as with Freud's life instinct, create a unity among persons, families, and nations, while death is the fate of those who have neglected such works of love and whose life, therefore, is an expression of that egoism which is divisive, which creates interpersonal barriers, and which manifests what Freud called the destructive or death instinct. In Freudian terms the goal of faith is the victory of life over death.

Freud himself, however, seems to have interpreted religious faith as a manifestation of the death instinct rather than in terms

THE PROBLEM OF GOD 137

of the "life" which the New Testament promises to the believer. This Freudian interpretation of religion as death can be inferred from his twofold description of religion as an "illusion" and as an obsessional neurosis.

1. Religion as an Illusion In Freud's view, it is because the adult individual is still subject to the whims of nature and fate that he retains some of the sense of helplessness which he experienced as an infant and child. And if he still feels helpless and impotent, then he still experiences the need for a father to love and protect him. Having outgrown his dependence on his human father, he finds in God a substitute father. Belief then is seen as a revival of the infantile state of helplessness, and such a belief is based not on objective evidence but on the wish for a father figure to protect the individual against the dangers of fate and nature. Consequently, he refers to such a belief as an "illusion" because its principal motive is wish fulfillment.[2]

Freud believed that because of this helplessness, religion was able to act as an agent of civilization by adding divine sanctions to the instinctual renunciation imposed by civilization, and it did so by teaching that cultural prohibitions have a divine origin. As with the child, the father who loves and protects also commands. Against such a view of religion Freud argues: that true religiousness does not consist in wallowing in one's helplessness and impotence but in seeking a remedy for them;[3] and that the future of civilization demands the dissociation of God from the precepts of civilization and the presentation of such precepts as the rational requirements of civilization (in other words, morality must become independent of belief in God).[4]

2. Religion as an Obsessional Neurosis Freud described the ontogenesis of religion in terms of the father-son relationship—a relationship characterized at first by dependence, but later, during the Oedipal stage, by ambivalent feelings of love and hate, trust and fear. As we have seen, the normal resolution of the Oedipus complex involves, on the part of the male child, a giving up of his sexual attraction to the mother and identification with the father. Since the father is perceived as both an ideal to be emulated and an obstacle to instinctual wishes, the child is torn by ambivalent feelings of love and hostility. The device used by the child to assist him in the repression of these hostile feelings is that of introjection, whereby the child, instead of associating the obstacle to his instincts with the father, reconstructs the obstacle within his own psychic apparatus in the form of the superego, which represents the paternal prohibitions incorporated within the child's own mind. The father obstacle is internalized in such a way that the prohibitions come from within—from conscience.[5] It is these repressed feelings of hostility which assert themselves through the agency of the superego, which directs that hostility towards one's own ego.

In Freud's opinion, failure to outgrow these ambivalent feelings towards one's father results in a lingering sense of guilt, which is the basis for religious beliefs and practices. If God is a substitute for one's father, then these ambivalent feelings are transferred to God. An obsessional neurosis develops in the form of endless ritualistic efforts to cover up or atone for the feelings of hostility towards God. Y. Masih interprets Freud's view in these words: "If God at bottom is an exalted father of one's infancy, then forever he would remain an object of love and hate. Therefore, every attempt will be made to cover the hate impulses by means of ritualistic acts, and this is what we find in religion. Religion is characterized by the rituals of prayers, fastings, observances of certain days and months, etc. . . . . For these reasons, Freud calls religion the universal obsessional neurosis of mankind, and conversely, regards obsessional neurosis as a distorted private religion of the individual neurotic person."[6]

On both counts—both as an illusion and as an obsessional neurosis—religion would appear, therefore, to be a manifestation of the death instinct. If Freud is correct, that is, if God is no more than a father substitute whose function is to protect us from the tensions and conflicts of life and to hold out to us an eternity of ultimate quiescence in which all such conflict ends, then faith in such a God is, as R. S. Lee has argued, a retreat from life and a surrender to the death instinct.[7] Moreover, if such a God is a father substitute and therefore the object of transferred feelings of hostility and guilt arising from an unresolved Oedipus complex, then religion is dependent for its existence on the presence of guilt and hostility, that is, on the presence of the aggressive, destructive ego instincts, which, as we have seen, are derivatives of the death instinct. Freud himself implies as much: "Whether one has killed one's father or has abstained from doing so is not really the decisive thing. One is bound to feel guilty in either case, for the sense of guilt is an expression of the conflict due to ambivalence, of the eternal struggle between Eros and the instinct of destruction and death.''[8]

That faith, therefore, which the believer sees as ''life'' is seen by Freud as a manifestation of or surrender to the death instinct. To resolve this contradiction it is necessary to recall from our discussion of the dynamics of faith (ch. 3) the distinction between authentic faith existence and ''mere'' religion. In this regard, Peter Homans' analysis of the Freudian notion of transference and its application to the formation of the God-image is helpful.[9] The process by which an individual creates a God who is a father substitute and towards whom he directs his repressed feelings of hostility and guilt may aptly be referred to as transference for it is similar to the process in which the patient directs or transfers unconscious attitudes to the analyst in the process of psychotherapy. Homans, therefore, refers to the God of whom Freud speaks as the ''transference God.'' Such a God is a projection of unresolved psychic conflicts, and, as Homans suggests, this God must be ''worked through,'' just as the transference between patient and analyst must be worked through.

Freud, in offering such a psychological interpretation of religion, looked for a psychological transformation of the person, namely, a liberation from the transference God. But this liberation or self-transcendence is precisely what the believer feels he has achieved through faith, for he has discovered what Tillich calls ''the God beyond God''; that is, he has discovered in the Gospel of grace a God beyond the transference God. It is not difficult to find an analogy between Freud's transference God and the God to whom one relates when standing ''under the law'' and before whom one feels obliged to justify oneself. Such a God is the God of law, ethics, ''religion,'' and moralism—a God who is a projection of the superego—and it is this God and this moralism which are transcended in faith. In our discussion of the dynamics of faith it was seen that this moralistic striving for self-justification before the transference God is a necessary preamble to faith; for only when the attempt at self-justification fails is one open to the divine possibility of justification as a gift or grace. This attempt at self-justification is what Barth called ''religion,'' and Homans suggests that Barth's description of revelation as the ''abolition of religion'' could be paraphrased as the ''abolition of the transference God.''

Within the context of Freudian theory, therefore, the dynam-

ics of faith involves a transcending of the transference God or superego God, for the moralistic striving by which one attempts to serve
such a God is a manifestation of the death instinct, since it is an
attempt to control or atone for the guilt feelings which arise from
repressed hostility towards the father and are transferred to God.
If the believer is to "enter into life," he must discover the God
beyond the superego God. As Homans remarks, Freud himself saw
the necessity of a moral courage which lies beyond the superego.
For the believer, that courage, as Tillich has pointed out,[10] is to
be found in faith existence, for by faith the believer achieves the
"courage of confidence," namely, the courage to affirm one's existence because it has been affirmed and accepted by the "ground
of Being." It is a courage based neither on oneself (e.g., on one's
moral and religious achievements) nor on one's world, but on the
love and acceptance which the Christian believes are proclaimed
in the event of Jesus Christ.

It is this experience of acceptance (justification) which relieves
one of the necessity of egoistic self-justification. In Freudian terms,
one is relieved of acting on motives inspired by the ego instincts,
or (ultimately) the death instinct, and thereby freed to live according
to the life instinct. One's concern is now for the object of one's
love and "good works," rather than the justification and salvation those good works might "earn." Liberated from such self-
preoccupation, the believer is free to commit himself to the personal
relationship of faith, which involves that openness to life, risk, and
uncertainty which is characteristic of the life instinct. Though Freud
described religion as regressive, it might be more accurate to
describe it as a necessary stage in the development of genuine faith.
One can transcend the superego God only by experiencing the futility of the moralistic striving for self-justification by which that God
is served. Nevertheless, Freud's use of the word *regression* is instructive, for genuine faith existence is a fragile possession and always
susceptible to the temptation to regress for reasons of security to
a moralistic and legalistic type of religion, as the history of Christian
morality attests. Ideally, the Christian believer is one who has transcended such moralism by discovering the God beyond the superego
God—a God, the revelation of whose love, forgiveness, and acceptance makes possible a faith relationship based on love rather than
on fear, guilt, and hostility; that is, on life rather than death.

The question now arises: Are we to deduce from the fore-
going discussion that the Freudian model of the God-image is irrel-

evant to Christian thought? Is there no possibility of a psychologically based natural theology in Freud's conclusions about the
psychological roots of religion? If the type of God-image and the
type of religion which result from the Oedipal experience represent
a necessary preamble to the development of authentic faith, then,
to this extent, the Freudian God-image has meaning for an understanding of the Christian faith experience. Left unanswered, however, is the question of whether any positive meaning can be
assigned to the father-image as a component of an authentic model
of transcendence. This brings us to the second major theme of
Freud's psychology of religion. The Freudian model of the God-
image appears inadequate not only because it implies a kind of religion which can be equated with death, but also because the image
of God as a substitute father appears to be excessively one-sided
and restricted: one-sided because it is based solely on the image
of the father to the near exclusion of the mother and others in the
child's environment; restricted in the sense that the meaning of
God and religion is discovered only in the Oedipal phase of human
development and in the father-son relationship. In terms of the
"question of natural theology" which we have been asking, the
human experience which gives rise to the question of God is, in
Freud's view, the ambivalent relationship with the father during
the Oedipal phase of growth. Before discussing the adequacy of
such a model for Christian thought, it will be helpful to mention
briefly some of the revisions and elaborations of that model to be
found within the psychoanalytic tradition.

One reason that can be advanced for the one-sidedness of
Freud's God-image is that it was elaborated within a particular
phylogenetic context. The ambivalent feelings of the son towards
his father in the Oedipal experience represented, for Freud, a re-
enactment of the killing of the father of the primal horde by his
sons, with the resulting guilt feelings and eventual deification of
the father.[11] Such a drama can only be relived and re-enacted in
reference to the father, and if this event and the racial memory
of it account for the origin and continuation of religion, then God
can only be the "exalted father." A recent study by Dr. Ana-Maria
Rizzuto makes use of clinical evidence to support the thesis that
the God-image is not based exclusively on the idea of the father
but results rather from the child's experiences with various "significant others" in his/her environment, including both parents, grand-
parents, or even imaginary figures. All these are possible compo-

nents of the individual's image of God through the process of object representation. "My study and present knowledge of object representations," she states, "make it impossible to accept that the paternal imago only is used to form the representation of God. The components of my patients' God representations came from varied sources, and although in most patients one source prevailed, no patient formed his God representation from only one parental imago."[12] The conclusion to which Rizzuto is led by her clinical experience is that "formation of the image of God does not depend upon the oedipal conflict," for "clinical cases show Gods belonging to each level of development from oral to oedipal."[13]

If we look upon Rizzuto's work as a revision of the Freudian model of the God-image, the thrust of that revision is twofold: the material for the mental representation of God comes from other figures in the child's environment and not just the father; and all childhood stages of development (oral, anal, Oedipal) contribute to the formation of the God-image. Among those who stress the relationship to the mother as a component of the God-image are Erik Erikson and Erich Fromm. Erikson is best known for his epigenetic schema of the eight developmental stages of the life cycle from infancy to old age. Within this developmental model the psychological roots of religion are primarily located in the first year of life. In Erikson's psychosocial elaboration of Freud's psychosexual model of development, this first, oral stage of growth is characterized by the conflict between "basic trust" and mistrust, and the role of the mother or mothering person is critical for a healthy resolution of this conflict. R. S. Lee speaks of the mother as "the bridge to the world"—the bridge by which we pass from infantile narcissism to an awareness of and relatedness to the external world.[14] For Erikson this means that the relationship to the mother is prototypical for the relationships one develops towards all of reality. The quality of that original relationship will determine in large part whether each subsequent relationship will be predominantly one of trust or mistrust.

Since trust is the formal element of faith, the child's growing sense of trust becomes the "raw material" of religious faith. Organized religion, in fact, represents for Erikson an "institutional safeguard" for the child's growing sense of trust.[15] It is the attitude of basic trust which is developed in relation to the mother which helps the individual to assimilate the insecurity of facing reality alone; or, as Erikson would have it, individual autonomy (the developmental task of the second stage of growth) must develop against the background of basic trust—trust in the willingness of the mother to help sustain the child in the face of the failures he encounters in his attempts at autonomous behaviour (e.g., walking). This same attitude of basic trust must sustain the adult in the face of life's negative experiences.[16] The attitude of basic trust which the infant directs towards the mother is experienced by the mature adult towards reality in general and by the religious person towards ultimate reality, that is, towards God. In this way, faith as trust results in a sense of ultimate security which is the basis for the "courage to be." In Erikson's understanding, therefore, the mother-image would be the primary component of the God-image, and the experience of the oral—not the Oedipal—phase of growth would be the primary psychological root of religion.[17]

Erich Fromm rejects Freud's sexual interpretation of the Oedipus complex in favour of an interpretation which invokes, not the sexual attraction to the parent of the opposite sex, but the human condition according to which the child of either sex experiences an *emotional* attachment to the mother. This emotional attachment takes the form of the certainty, security, and unconditional love which the child experiences within the "emotional orbit" of the mother. The emotional dependence on the mother, which provides the child with a sense of belonging or "rootedness," must be given up, however, for the sake of a new kind of rootedness which the mature person achieves through "productive relatedness" or "brotherliness." These terms refer to a form of relatedness to others in which one's individuality and integrity are preserved. Human growth involves an exchange: one must give up the certainty and security of dependence on the mother and accept the risk and insecurity which accompany that independence or autonomy which is the goal of human becoming. The "giving up" of the mother, therefore, is not the result of the presence of father-rival but of the demands of life and of normal human growth.[18]

Fromm believed that Freud's distortion of the theory of the Oedipus complex was due largely to the patriarchal attitude of Freud's own times. If we reject an exclusively sexual interpretation of the Oedipus complex, he argues, then the attachment to the mother can be seen as having a positive character as well as the negative, pathological character which Freud assigned to the incestuous fixation. One may therefore speak of a mother complex and a father complex, both having positive and negative characteristics and providing the experiential prototypes for the matriarchal and patriarchal features found in social structures and religions. The positive features of the attachment to the mother and of matriarchal structures are described as "a sense of affirmation of life, freedom and equality," while its negative features consist of "being bound to nature, to blood and soil," with the result that "man is blocked from developing his individuality and his reason." The positive aspects of the father complex are identified as "reason, discipline, conscience and individualism," while the negative aspects are "hierarchy, oppression, inequality, submission."[19]

Since the relationship of the child to the father "does not have the same intensity as that to the mother, because the father never has the all-enveloping, all-protective, all-loving role which the mother has for the first years of the child's life," there is a different quality to the paternal and maternal relationships. "While the mother represents nature and unconditional love, the father represents abstraction, conscience, duty, law and hierarchy."[20] While the mother's love is unconditional, the father's love tends to be conditional and demanding. This distinction allows Fromm to revise Freud's concept of conscience. Conscience is not only the internalized voice of the father issuing commands and prohibitions, for "there is not only a fatherly but also a motherly conscience; there is a voice which tells us to do our duty, and a voice which tells us to love and to forgive—others as well as ourselves."[21] Conscience, therefore, has a paradoxical quality, offering us conflicting criteria which must somehow be reconciled in making moral decisions: "Father's and mother's voices speak a different language: in fact they seem to say opposite things, yet the contradiction between the principle of duty and the principle of love, of fatherly and motherly conscience, is a contradiction inherent in human existence, and both sides of the contradiction must be accepted."[22] This tension or paradox of which Fromm speaks is evident in the Christian understanding of God, who is seen as being at the same time a God of duty and of love, of law and of grace. It is also revealed in the paradoxical nature of faith by which the believer sees himself as *simul justus et peccator*—as sinner because he stands under God's demanding law, and yet as justified or accepted because he stands under God's unconditional love or grace. In terms, therefore, of our question about the psychological roots of the God-image, any corrective to the one-sidedness of Freudian theory must point to the mother figure as a component of the Christian God-image.

The importance of the role of both mother and father in the formation of the Christian God-image and in the religious development of the child is further developed by Heije Faber. The working hypothesis of his book *Psychology of Religion* is that "the bond with the mother—and we would add, with the father—is of essential importance for religious development."[23] On this premise he constructs a schema of religious development based on the Freudian stages of growth as elaborated particularly by Erikson. For Faber, each stage of human growth—oral, anal, Oedipal, etc.—represents the emergence of a pattern of adaptation which becomes prototypical for later patterns of cultural and religious adaptation. Thus the contrast between the oral and anal stages represents the contrast between a mode of adaptation characterized by oneness with and participation in the mother and one characterized by individuality, autonomy, and achievement. These modes of adaptation are prototypical for certain religious modes of adaptation and represent for Faber the psychological and developmental basis for the distinction between naturalistic and prophetic-historical types of religion. The God of naturalistic religion represents an original unity and is seen as a projection of the mother-image, while the creator, lawgiver God of historical-prophetic religion is seen as a projection of the father-image. And just as the child's attempts at autonomy must be carried out against a background of basic trust towards the mother, in the same way, Faber believes, the religious pattern of obedience and achievement must be built on the foundation of participation in and oneness with God. The anxiety of separation is overcome by a sense of participation. Faber suggests that where autonomy develops without a sufficient background of basic trust the resulting religious pattern of adaptation may be characterized by an excessive striving for self-justification as in Pharisaism, or in a compulsive type of moral purity and achievement as in Puritanism, or in a complete loss of the religious dimension of life as in the process of secularization.[24]

Faber states that "the believer's picture of God reflects a pattern derived from his own development, because he cannot do anything else than project onto his God the feelings about particular key figures which emerge in the course of this development.''[25] But the Christian picture of God is, as we have seen, paradoxical, combining unconditional love and acceptance with ethical demands. One's relationship with this God does not follow the extremes of either the oral pattern (complete dependence and participation) or of the anal pattern (separation, autonomy, and achievement). This accounts, in Faber's view, for the significance of the third, Oedipal phase, for this phase introduces a new type of relationship which becomes the pattern for a different kind of relationship with God. At this stage the child's relationship to the father becomes important, and it is a different kind of relationship from that experienced with the mother. The father is a more remote figure. The child does not separate himself from an original oneness with the father as he did with mother; he encounters the father as a third person in the triangle—a person who, like God, has the quality of ''otherness.'' Any sense of oneness or participation which the child experiences with the father must be experienced, in Faber's words, ''beyond the cleft of a detachment.'' Father and son ''are not to be understood as a totality, like mother and son. And if the relationship is a totality at all, it is different from the one shared with the mother, more a question of doing things together, of companionship, rather than being together.''[26]

This relationship in which there is experienced both a bond and a detachment is therefore an experiential prototype for the experience of the Christian God and a pattern for the paradoxical Christian God-image. In light of this, it would appear that Freud was right—or at least consistent with Christian thought—in pointing to the father-child relationship as the key to an understanding of God and religion. He erred, however, in reducing the paradoxical nature of that relationship to a simple guilt-producing contradiction between love for the loving, protecting father and hostility towards the commanding father. As Faber has pointed out, the father-child relationship is an ''I-Thou'' relationship combining both distance and participation. It is therefore the prototypical pattern for a God-image combining both transcendence and immanence and for a type of religion which combines both ethics and mysticism, trust and autonomy, independence and dependence.

While Freud saw religion as a regressive infantile illusion or as an obsessional neurosis—that is, as opposed to the goal of mature personality growth—Jung saw the language and imagery

of religion as symbolic ways of expressing the human striving for
wholeness or selfhood. Indeed, Jung's psychological writings
abound with "religious" terminology. Terms such as "soul,"
"rebirth," "reconciliation," and "crucifixion of the ego" are used
to express psychological realities and processes. If the goal of personality growth is the overcoming of one-sidedness and the achieving
of wholeness—a movement, that is, from incompleteness to completeness, from inauthentic to authentic human existence—then
it is experienced as a kind of "rebirth." For Jung, therefore, the
religious language of rebirth expressed in a symbolic way the goal
of the process of human becoming, a process which Jung termed
"individuation."

It must be remembered, however, that Jung's positive attitude towards religion is methodologically limited to religion's
symbolic or psychological value. In this context, religion is valuable
to the extent that its dogmas, rituals, and symbols correlate with
the archetypal motifs of the unconscious and direct our growth
towards the assimilation of such archetypal material into conscious
life and, therefore, towards greater wholeness. The God-image,
for example, is in Jung's view a symbol of totality or wholeness
corresponding to the archetype of the self. It thus has meaning for
human existence, or, in Jung's words, it is "psychologically real."
Jung tries to remain neutral about the metaphysical truth claims
of religion—with what degree of success seems to be a matter of
debate among students of Jung—and about the value of organized
religion. Consider this famous passage from his 1932 essay "Psychotherapists or the Clergy":

> Among all my patients in the second half of life—
> that is to say, over thirty-five—there has not been one
> whose problem in the last resort was not that of find-
> ing a religious outlook on life. It is safe to say that
> every one of them fell ill because he had lost that which
> the living religions of every age have given to their
> followers, and none of them has been really healed
> who did not regain his religious outlook.[27]

The "religious outlook" of which Jung speaks does not refer to
belief in certain religious doctrines. It refers to what Jung, in the
same essay, calls an "attitude of unprejudiced objectivity" by which

one "senses in everything the unseen presence of the divine will"
(*CW*, 11:520). Such an attitude, he explains, relativizes our conventional judgements about the evil we perceive in ourselves and
others because it senses the presence of a superior power at work.
"The truly religious person has this attitude," Jung maintains,
and consequently, a more accepting attitude towards one's "dark
side" and that of others since God "seeks in the most curious ways
to enter a man's heart" (*CW*, 11:520). The religious outlook, therefore, is a fundamental awareness and acceptance of a superior power
beyond one's controlling and judging ego, or what Jung elsewhere
describes as "certain dynamic factors, that are conceived as
'powers' " (*CW*, 11:8)—whether those powers are understood as
religious realities or as archetypes of the collective unconscious.
Religion, for Jung, is the experience of such powers; creeds are
"codified and dogmatized forms" of such experience (*CW*, 11:509).
Edward Edinger remarks that such an experience is an experience
of "the infinite" in which "the Ego is relativized. It acknowledges
a supraordinate authority and experiences itself *sub specie aeternita-
lis.*"[28] The "living religions of every age" are of value insofar as
they have promoted, through their symbol systems, this type of
experience. Lest we forget that Jung is speaking of this psychological
function of religion only, he is quick to remind us in the words
which immediately follow the above excerpt. "This of course,"
he says, "has nothing whatever to do with a particular creed or
membership of a church" (*CW*, 11:509).

Jung's understanding of religion is evident in those features
of the individuation process which he emphasized in speaking of
that process as a "religious quest." As we have already seen, Jung
saw religion as having the same goal as the individuation process.
Salvation and *rebirth* were, for Jung, religious words whose meanings
were analogous to those of the psychological terms *wholeness* or *selfhood*. Religious images of rebirth were seen as symbols which related
meaningfully to the archetype of the self in the human psyche. Religion, therefore, expresses the desire for rebirth or wholeness in a
symbolic way, that is, through symbols, ritual, dogma, and myth
onto which the archetypes of the collective unconscious are projected. The story of creation and the fall, for example, expresses
in a symbolic and mythical way—the expulsion from paradise—
the consequences of the growth of consciousness. The paradise from
which we have been cast out is the unconscious from which con-

sciousness has separated us. It then becomes the religious and psychological task to overcome this state of separation and isolation, and to recover the lost unity through the reunion of consciousness and the unconscious. This kind of rebirth through reimmersion in the unconscious is aptly expressed in the symbolism of the baptismal liturgy.

The religious nature of the individuation process is reflected in the words of Charles Hanna, who maintains that "salvation, health, and wholeness depend upon the recovery on a higher level of this lost unity and harmony. Such recovery is the primary concern of both religion and psychology."[29] The linking of the words "salvation, health, and wholeness" is significant, for it reflects the Jungian view that the goal of individuation is identical with the religious desire for rebirth. In Jung's view, then, the primary goal of religion is that inner rebirth or transformation which results in the experience of personal wholeness. Whereas Freud was concerned with the ethical, social, and cultural functions of religion, Jung saw religion as primarily an inner, psychological experience and only secondarily as a sociological and historical phenomenon. Jung may or may not have overstepped the boundaries of his discipline and dealt directly with metaphysical questions. What is more important, I believe, for an understanding of his approach to religion is that Jung not only restricted himself to the study of religion as a psychological phenomenon, but he seems also to have considered questions of the historical and metaphysical truth of religion to be *less important* than its psychological truth. This means that for Jung the question of the objective metaphysical truth of a dogma is less important than the dogma's symbolic function in relation to unconscious archetypes; God as the archetype of totality is more important than God as an objective existing reality; Christ as a symbol of the self is more important than the historical Christ; experience is more important than faith. Jung obviously believes he is getting to the heart of the matter when he says of the notion of divinely inspired dreams (and by implication of any religious belief): "When an idea is so old and so generally believed, it must be true in some way, by which I mean that it is psychologically true" (*CW*, 5:4).

In his book *Jung and St. Paul* David Cox attempted to draw a parallel between the conflict which St. Paul describes between conscious good will and evil inclinations and the tension which Jung speaks of as existing between the conscious and unconscious dimensions of one's personality. As we have seen, this state of antagonism, separation, and conflict is for Jung the "fallen" state from which we must be saved and therefore the object of both psychological and religious healing. Cox suggests that for both Jung and St. Paul this healing or salvation takes place when the individual ceases to rely on his own will. When he does so, something *happens* to him and he comes to a way of living which is directed by a "centre" which is not identical with the conscious ego.[30] Whatever the merits of such an analogy between Jung and St. Paul, it is certainly true that Jung laid particular emphasis on certain observable aspects of the human search for wholeness.

In the first place, Jung believed that Western man, in particular, suffered from the alienation of consciousness from its unconscious depths, and therefore from the illusion of identifying himself with his ego consciousness and of believing that he was in conscious control of his own life. Against such an illusion Jung pointed out that our emotions, moods, and dreams seem to have a life of their own, and we cannot command them to come or go. Even our thoughts sometimes take on an obsessive character which puts them beyond the control of our will (*CW*, 8:667). This "concern with consciousness at the expense of the unconscious" means a loss of contact with one's unconscious roots (since consciousness grows out of unconscious life), and the individual ends by "putting his own conception of himself in place of his real being" (*CW*, 10:557). It means, further, that we suffer from the prejudice of believing that the contents of the psyche represent our own doing— that we are responsible for and makers of our psychic condition. In *Psychology and Religion* Jung uses the example of a patient suffering from the morbid obsession—contrary to all physical evidence— that he has cancer. The patient considers himself somehow responsible for this morbid imagination, whereas if he had a real cancer, he would feel no such responsibility. In that case, the cancer would be seen as something which merely *happened* to him (*CW*, 11:12–20).

Furthermore, Jung considered this prejudice to be of relatively recent origin, and, contrary to it, he believed that psychic events and conditions such as the morbid cancer idea—as well as sudden irrational moods, dreams, and phantasies—are often things which *happen* to us. We are not the creators of such psychic conditions. Jung's theoretical explanation of this is to be found, again, in his understanding of the individuation process, which he believed was directed by the unconscious in an autonomous way. Dreams, phantasies, complexes, and obsessions are thereby subject to inter-pretation as statements about the individual's spiritual or psycho-logical condition which originate in the unconscious. Jung's judge-ment, therefore, about the cancer obsession is that it is "a spontaneous growth which originated in the part of the psyche that is not identical with consciousness. It appears to be an autonomous formation intruding upon consciousness" (*CW*, 11:21). Such intru-sions, because they do not originate in consciousness, are expe-rienced as emanating from an objective source. Indeed, Jung describes the unconscious as the "objective psyche," and the indi-viduation process is seen as a series of encounters with the objective psyche. The belief in ghosts, witches, demons, angels, and gods—as well as belief in the soul as an objective reality—Jung considered to be projections onto objective external agents of what was in fact the autonomous activity of an objective, inner agent, the uncon-scious psyche. This kind of projection, he believed, was neverthe-less closer to the truth than is the modern tendency to see such psychic events in purely subjective terms and to see ourselves as creators of our own dreams and phantasies, "for not only on the primitive level, but with civilized man as well, psychic happenings have an objective side" (*CW*, 8:667).

Here again we encounter the religious character of the indi-viduation process. If the unconscious acts in a way that is inde-pendent of consciousness, then it is experienced as having a "numinous" quality. Jung defines religion, with Rudolf Otto, as the experience of the "numinosum," which he further defines as "certain dynamic factors, that are conceived as 'powers': spirits, demons, gods, laws, ideas, ideals or whatever name man has given to such factors in his world as he has found powerful, dangerous or helpful enough to be taken into careful consideration, or grand, beautiful and meaningful enough to be devoutly worshipped and loved" (*CW*, 11:8). Like the unconscious, the numinous is "a dynamic agency or effect not caused by an arbitrary act of will" which "seizes and controls the human subject, who is always rather its victim than its creator" (*CW*, 11:6). Religion, like the individ-uation process, creates "an attitude peculiar to a consciousness which has been changed by experience of the numinosum" (*CW*, 11:9).

Finally, the individuation process is a personal quest which suffers when the individual is swallowed up in the mass. Individuation represents "the goal and meaning of individual life," and it is this goal and meaning which suffer when the individual is dehumanized by mass movements, philosophical abstractions, and the scientific, statistical world view which "thrusts aside the individual in favour of anonymous units that pile up into mass formations" (*CW*, 10:499). Religion, on the other hand, is seen as the "counterbalance to mass-mindedness." Here Jung has in mind that kind of religion which, like the individuation process, is concerned with the goal and meaning of individual life and has the same goal of personal transformation and the experience of wholeness. For this reason, Jung is careful to distinguish genuine religion from "creed." "A creed," he says, "gives expression to a definite collective belief, whereas the word *religion* expresses a subjective relationship to certain metaphysical extramundane factors" (*CW*, 10:507). The essence of true religion, therefore, lies in the personal relationship with the deity which is unique to each individual, while a creed represents a levelling process in which all the members collectively subscribe to the same doctrine and the same rules of moral conduct. While religion represents an original transforming experience of the numinous, "creeds are codified and dogmatized forms of original religious experience" (*CW*, 11:10). This is not to deny the potential value of the organized religious community, but the value of that community is ultimately dependent on the personal religious experience of the individual members. "Just as the addition of however many zeroes," Jung argues, "will never make a unit, so the value of a community depends on the spiritual and moral stature of the individuals composing it" (*CW*, 10:516).

To summarize: the individuation process has a "religious" quality in that (1) it shares with religion the goal of personal transformation and the achieving of wholeness or selfhood; (2) it involves an encounter with the unconscious which is experienced as an objective reality (the "objective psyche") just as religious experience involves the experience of the numinous; and (3) it is an intensely personal quest which, like religion, is hindered by mass-mindedness.

We may now summarize the different ways in which Freud and Jung analyze the psychological roots of the God-image. In Jungian theory the archetype of the self, since it represents wholeness or totality, correlates with a notion of a God who, like the God discovered in Tillich's ontological method, represents the totality of being, the principle or ground of being in which every particular being participates just as every individual consciousness is grounded in humanity's collective unconscious. This type of God-image correlates in turn with the traditional understanding of natural or naturalistic religion, whose characteristics might be summarized as follows:

1. An emphasis on mystical participation in the all-embracing total-ity of God or nature
2. An emphasis on the importance of the mother-image since the original oneness with the mother is the psychological prototype for such participation
3. A view of nature as symbolic of the inner experience of rebirth

As John E. Smith has pointed out,[31] natural religion attempts to transcend history and derive knowledge of God from what is timeless and universal. If the concept of God can be derived, for example, from a religious dimension of human personality, such as the self archetype, then this concept becomes the common possession of humanity and not the special prerogative of a chosen group to whom it has been revealed.

In Freudian theory the relationship with the father correlates with the concept of God as the transcendent other—a personal God who is not the principle or ground of being but the Supreme Being. Perhaps we may say more accurately, with Emmanuel Levinas,[32] that such a God is not identified with the totality of being but with that which transcends the totality, namely, with a concept of infinity. Again, this concept of God correlates with a particular type of religion—revealed or prophetic-historical religions, in which the following characteristics are evident:

1. An emphasis on revelation which establishes a bond in spite of the distance which separates the human and the divine
2. An emphasis on the importance of the father-image since the relationship to the father is the psychological prototype for a relationship with God combining distance and participation
3. An emphasis on ethical responsibility rather than mystical participation

Again, as John E. Smith has pointed out,[33] revealed religion is rooted in the historical disclosure of God. God reveals himself, not through the natural world or human nature, but through historical

events and an historical founder. The result is not an awareness
of the "generalized holy," but a definite conception of God which,
in turn, is not the common possession of humanity but of a community of faith which is the bearer of that revelation.

In discussing the psychological roots of the God-image, Freud
and Jung point to two types of experience which correlate with two
different types of religion and two different concepts of God. Gordon
Kaufman has described these two approaches to the question of
God as the "interpersonal" and the "teleological" models of transcendence.[34] These are two types of human experience which
serve as models for an understanding of divine transcendence.
Teleological transcendence is based on the human experience of
the self as an agent acting to realize certain goals. The end sought
transcends the present experience of the self and is based, therefore, on the experience of the self as incomplete. This model would
correspond to the Jungian model of religious experience as the individual self seeking to overcome the narrowness of ego-consciousness
and to experience a rebirth to wholeness or selfhood. It corresponds
also to what Kaufman calls a "theology of being" in which all finite
beings are seen as grounded in and striving towards God as the
ultimate reality in which they essentially participate. This ultimate
reality is not viewed anthropomorphically, but ethically as the ultimate good, aesthetically as perfect beauty, and intellectually as being
itself or the ground of being.[35]

Interpersonal transcendence is derived from the human experience of interpersonal life, namely, our experience and knowledge
of other persons. This knowledge is derived not so much from the
self's striving for a goal; nor is it like the knowledge we have of
"things," which depends on what we do to obtain knowledge.
Knowledge of other persons depends more on what they do, that
is, on their honesty in communicating and thereby revealing themselves—a communication which is theirs to give or to withhold.
The inaccessibility of the other apart from his self-revelation reflects
the meaning of "transcendence" as referring to that which is beyond
our power to control. This model of transcendence implies a personal God as opposed to the more impersonal notion of "Being."
God is seen as more independent from our world because he is an
autonomous agent. Nevertheless, he is viewed more anthropomorphically "since in our finite experience only persons enjoy this kind
of fully objective transcendence."[36]

Tillich argues that the ontological method is necessary in the philosophy of religion to counterbalance the anthropomorphism of the cosmological method—and, we might add, of the interpersonal model of transcendence. When theology is not complemented by ontology, it "speaks of God as of a being beside others, subject to the structure of being as all beings are, stars and men and animals, the highest being but not being itself."[37] Such a "being beside others" is, in Tillich's view, a concrete religious symbol for the only adequate object of ultimate concern—being itself. In other words, to conceive of God as a being, or in terms of the interpersonal model of transcendence, does not do justice to divine transcendence. Though this may hold true within the confines of our traditional understanding of natural theology (i.e., that the cosmological method needs to be complemented by the ontological method), the theologian must take into account that Christianity is a revealed religion. From the theological point of view, therefore, all forms of "general" revelation—including concepts of God derived from the ontological method, the teleological model of transcendence, or any method in which the meaning of God is derived from the conditions of finite existence—must be completed by "special" revelation or God's own self-disclosure. And, in the Christian perspective, the mode of this revelation is personal. "In the Christian understanding of revelation," writes John E. Smith, "God stands to those to whom he is revealed in a relationship that is analogous to the situations in which two selves encounter each other."[38]

In this context the interpersonal becomes the more adequate model of transcendence in spite of its anthropomorphism, as Kaufman argues:

It is somewhat curious that the more anthropomorphic of the two models (and thus the one that seems to imply that God is most like us and presumably most easily knowable by us) is at the same time the model with which a more unqualified kind of divine transcendence can be affirmed. For here God is the impenetrable mystery, known only in and through his revelation in concrete historical events. In contrast the model of transcendence that eschews anthropomorphisms of all sorts and regards God simply as *Being*

turns out to be the one in which God is less hidden
and less mysterious. For with teleological transcendence the fittingness or correspondence of the transcendent goal to the striving of the finite self is always
implied, and with it a certain proportionality between
the experienced finite order and the Infinite.[39]

The premise of the interpersonal model of transcendence is that
God is apprehended only in the course of interpersonal history.
It correlates, therefore, with historical theologies of revelation and
leaves "no real place for a natural theology in the usual sense."[40]
In the light, however, of our understanding of the "new style"
of natural theology, Kaufman's interpersonal model of transcendence can be seen as an exercise in natural theology for it points
to a dimension of human existence (interpersonal life), not as
proving God's existence, but as correlating with what theology says
about God and his self-disclosure.

Freud, in pointing to the father-child relationship as the
psychological root of religion, is, distortions notwithstanding, closer
to this model than is Jung. The Freudian model points to the concept of a God who reveals himself over a distance and does so
through persons and events. This is closer to the definite conception of God derived from historical theologies of revelation than
the awareness of what Smith calls the "generalized holy," which
derives from a religious dimension of human existence or human
personality such as the Jungian self archetype. I have argued in
chapter 5 that Jung's analysis of the correlation between conscious
God-images and the unconscious archetype of selfhood or wholeness represents a restatement of the ontological argument, but
within the confines of a revised understanding of natural theology.
As natural theology, however, it falls within that model of transcendence which we have been calling ontological or teleological
and correlates with an image of God as ground of being or all-
embracing totality.

Within the context of the new style of natural theology, this
model of transcendence, which begins with the self as incomplete
and on the basis of a correlation or proportionality between the
finite order and the infinite, between the striving of the finite self
and its transcendent goal, proceeds to an awareness of the "generalized holy," must be considered incomplete. Since Christianity

is a revealed religion, this teleological model must be completed, as we have seen, by the interpersonal model of transcendence. In the light of revelation, the relationship with God is what Martin Buber called an "I-Thou" relationship with a face-to-face being, as opposed to an "I-it" relationship with a passive object. Buber argued that philosophical systems which account for God in terms of subjective experience contribute to the "eclipse of God." They destroy the truly interpersonal nature of the religious relationship because "they can no longer endure a God who is not confined to man's subjectivity, who is not merely a 'supreme value.' "[41] We can speak of a truly religious relationship only when the object of philosophical speculation—"unlimited Being"—becomes personalized. "I-Thou finds its highest intensity and transfiguration in religious reality, in which unlimited Being becomes, as absolute person, my partner."[42]

In the context of our discussion this means that the Jungian account of the psychological roots of the God-image must be completed by the Freudian account. The experience of the archetype of the self is the experiential prototype for a God-image representing totality and for a theology of being. As we have seen, the I-Thou relationship to the father, combining both participation and distance, is the experiential prototype for an interpersonal model of transcendence and an historical theology of revelation. The task, therefore, of a psychologically based natural theology would be to investigate the correlation between the Christian symbol system (including the God-image) with the experience of both the archetype of the self and the relationship with the father. For the believer, there need not be any contradiction between the revealed character of Christianity and the "natural religiousness" of the human person; the God of whom he is naturally aware as the "generalized holy" or the numinous is revealed as person in Christ. Since our thinking is not restricted to the categories of traditional natural theology, this does not refer to a simple reversion to the cosmological method—a substitution of supreme being for being itself, of rational demonstration for immediate awareness—for the medium of revelation is, in this case, a person.

As John E. Smith has pointed out, the Christian understanding of God falls between the "mystical view," in which knowledge of God is a matter of immediate awareness independent of all media of knowledge, and the "rationalistic view," in which knowledge of God is by inference from the existence of other things, that is, through media of disclosure. Both of these approaches attempt to transcend history and base the knowledge of God on what is timeless and universal. Christianity, Smith argues, makes central what is neglected in these two approaches by looking to history and historical events as "media for the disclosure of God." Since media of disclosure are involved, this is not a mystical view; nor is it rationalistic since, through the medium, God is directly but not immediately experienced and encountered. "If we can understand how a self can be directly present to another self and yet require a medium or form of expression through which disclosure takes place, we shall have some idea of what the revelation of God means."[43] This mode of disclosure is required, Smith argues, because God is neither an immediate quality to be known through immediate awareness nor a universal character to be known through the medium of concepts. As a person or self, God is directly present to us but must be revealed through word and gesture.[44]

The question we have been dealing with may be summarized as follows: Which God-image is the more adequate image of ultimate reality: the God-image representing an all-embracing totality in which individual beings participate and of which the self archetype is the experiential prototype; or the God-image representing a person or self to whom one is related from a distance and of which the experiential prototype is the I-Thou relationship to the father? As we have seen, Tillich identifies God with this all-embracing totality, with being as such or the ground of being, and argues that divine transcendence is thereby preserved since God is removed from the category of "a being beside others." This all-embracing ground of being is the "God beyond God," the necessary counterbalance to the anthropomorphism of the various religious images of God and to the hazard of "supranaturalism" in traditional theism. Against this I have argued that, in view of the revealed nature of Christianity, the interpersonal model of transcendence must complement and complete the ontological or teleological model. And, in doing so, we do not step outside the bounds of natural theology if we accept the new understanding of natural theology as dealing with the dimensions of human experience which correlate with theological concepts.

The question arises: Does the interpersonal model of transcendence appear more adequate only in the light of positive theology and the revealed character of Christianity, or can it be argued on strictly philosophical grounds? The answer to this question is beyond the scope of our discussion. However, our discussion would not be complete without some reference to how this general position is stated by Emmanuel Levinas. In his book *Totality and Infinity* Levinas distinguishes between "ontology," which locates ultimate meaning and reality in an all-embracing totality that absorbs the individuality of the many, and "metaphysics," which locates ultimate meaning and reality in what transcends the whole or totality, namely, the infinite. Totality and infinity, therefore, may be seen again as two models of transcendence, and Levinas identifies God or that which is truly transcendent with the infinite. Religion, therefore, is identified not with ontology but with "metaphysical desire." Ontological desire is the desire to return to or be reunited with that reality of which we are essentially a part; it is the desire for totality, which, we might add, is analogous to the psychological desire for wholeness. Metaphysical desire, on the other hand, is the desire for the other; it is not desire for simply another being, for "alterity," but for that which is "absolutely other," namely, infinity.

What is desired metaphysically is neither an object of need which one can possess and which therefore satisfies or completes one; nor is it a desire to return to that reality of which one is essentially a part. It is the desire for "something else entirely," and if religion is an expression of metaphysical desire, then religion is "the bond that is established between the same and the other without constituting a totality."[45] Ontology does not do justice to the idea of transcendence because concepts like the "ground of being" destroy the polarity between self and other, subordinate the relationship with an existent someone (the ethical relationship) to a relationship with the "being of the existent," and thereby subordinate ethics to freedom, for ethical responsibility is responsibility to the truly other.[46] Transcendence is seen to be linked more fittingly to the idea of infinity. The infinite is the "absolutely other" which transcends any ideas one might have of it. It is therefore not the object of natural religion but must be revealed, not the object of cognition but of desire. Levinas distinguishes this metaphysical/religious desire from ontological need, for "desire is an aspiration that the Desirable animates; it originates from its 'object'; it is a revelation—whereas need is a void of the soul; it proceeds from the subject."[47]

In Levinas' view, therefore, the transcendent is to be dis-

tinguished from that totality with which we seek union by participation. That which is truly transcendent can only be revealed, and
revelation implies a separated existent, just as, in interpersonal life,
the other must reveal himself over the distance that separates
persons. But to receive this revelation is not to know the source
as an object but rather "to be in relation with a substance overflow-
ing its own idea in me,"[48] just as one can never objectify another
person on the basis of his self-revelation. Interpersonal life and the
religious, ethical relationship, therefore, represent the most adequate
model of transcendence:

> Everything that cannot be reduced to an interhuman
> relation represents not the superior form but the for-
> ever primitive form of religion. . . . Totality and the
> embrace of being, or ontology, do not contain the final
> secret of being. Religion, where relationship subsists
> between the same and the other despite the impossibil-
> ity of the Whole—the idea of Infinity—is the ultimate
> structure.[49]

Whereas Tillich sees the fallen human condition as a condition of
existential separation from that to which we essentially belong, the
ground of being, Levinas argues that to interpret separation as a
"rupture of totality" is to interpret it exclusively in terms of *need*.
This implies that the separated being "does not entirely possess
its own being" and is therefore not truly separate.[50]

   Levinas mentions two aspects of Christianity which reinforce
the concept of infinity as a model of transcendence and point to
a God beyond totality: eschatology, and creation *ex nihilo*. Eschatology implies a relationship to a God beyond the totality or beyond
history. It is described as "a relationship with a surplus always
exterior to the totality, as though the objective totality did not fill
out the true measure of being, as though another concept, the concept of *infinity*, were needed to express this transcendence with
regard to totality, non-encompassable within a totality and as
primordial as totality."[51] If eschatology implies that reality has a
meaning "without a context," that is, a meaning which comes from
beyond the totality, the concept of creation *ex nihilo* implies that
the separated and created being is not merely an emanation from
God but something absolutely other than him. The idea of creation

conveys the idea of "a multiplicity not united into a totality"; it implies a dependent being, but not the dependence of a part separated from an original unity. Creation "posits a being outside of every system," for "what is essential to created existence is its separation with regard to the infinite."[52]

Whereas ontology sees the relationship to being itself as essentially one of participation—though a participation perhaps ruptured by the "fall"—metaphysics sees separation as an essential quality of the relationship to the infinite. Transcendence implies a relation over a distance—a relation with a totally other—"yet without this distance destroying this relation and without this relation destroying this distance, as would happen with relations with the same."[53] This is the kind of relationship implied in the concept of creation:

> For the idea of totality, in which the ontological philosophy veritably reunites—or comprehends—the multiple, must be substituted the idea of a separation resistant to synthesis. To affirm origin from nothing by creation is to contest the prior community of all things within eternity, from which philosophical thought, guided by ontology, makes things arise as from a common matrix. The absolute gap of separation which transcendence implies could not be better expressed than by the term creation, in which the kinship of beings among themselves is affirmed, but at the same time their radical heterogeneity also, their reciprocal exteriority coming from nothingness.[54]

I have suggested that the relationship to the father, in which there is combined a bond of unity with the aspect of distance or separation, is the experiential prototype for this model of transcendence and what Levinas calls the relationship to the infinite of which separation is an essential feature. It is a relationship in which freedom and uniqueness are preserved, and for this reason Levinas agrees that the relationship to the father constitutes an archetypal pattern for such a relationship. "The son resumes the unicity of the father," he points out, "and yet remains exterior to the father: the son is a unique son. Not by number; each son of the father is the unique son, the chosen, the chosen son. The love of the father for the son accomplishes the sole relation possible with the very unicity of another; and in this sense every love must approach paternal love."[55]

In evaluating the manner in which Freud and Jung analyze the psychological roots of the God-image, we should note that both models of transcendence we have been discussing are evident in Christian thought. The Christian God is conceived of philosophically as both all-embracing totality and as the totally other infinite; theologically, as both immanent and transcendent; and, we may add, psychologically, as both a projection of the archetype of self or totality and as a projection of the father-image. The Freudian notion of God as the exalted image of the father is not to be discarded; for by rooting the God-image in the child's first encounter with a truly "other" in his life, it preserves the idea of the divine-human relationship as interpersonal, that is, as combining distance and participation and as dependent on divine self-disclosure. As R. S. Lee has suggested,[56] the child at the Oedipal stage of growth, having differentiated himself from the original oneness with the mother, begins to develop a relationship with the father, whose image must first be differentiated from the mother rather than from himself. This means that in the resulting triangular relationship the father remains more alien and remote than the mother, and this "otherness" of the father is prototypical of the otherness or transcendence of God.

It could be argued, on the other hand, that in the Jungian perspective transcendence or "otherness" is implied in the numinous quality of the experience of the God/self archetype. In this case, however, what is experienced, while it is "other" than the conscious ego, is nevertheless continuous with one's true or total self. The transcendent, therefore, is identified with a totality of which one is part. What is *experienced* as "other" or numinous is in fact continuous with the deepest dimension of the self. Hence Jung's contention that, at the experiential level, the God-image and images of the self are indistinguishable. If this be the case, then there is room for another model of transcendence which, as Levinas suggests, describes the transcendent as infinite or "totally other," that is, as existing beyond this totality.

From the perspective of Christian theology, these two conflicting models of transcendence—or, in the context of this discussion, conflicting explanations of the psychological roots of the God-image—need not present us with an "either/or" choice. As we have seen, the Christian God-image is itself a paradoxical juxtaposition of two conflicting images. Theologically, both models of transcendence are valid. God is both all-encompassing totality and the totally other infinite; both the God of grace and the God of law; both unconditionally accepting and unconditionally demanding; both immanent and transcendent. To experience such a God, therefore, is to experience oneself as, in Luther's paradoxical phrase, *simul justus et peccator*. To have faith in such a God is not to dissolve one image into the other or to synthesize them but, in keeping with what Jung has to say about the transcendent function of symbols, to transcend the conflict and to see the opposing images as somehow belonging together.

I would argue that the new style of natural theology is more than a religious anthropology which attempts to account for the human awareness of transcendence in general (Smith's "generalized holy"). It also seeks to explain the human meaning of what positive theology accepts as the specific contents of God's "special" revelation to an historical community in an historical time, place, and person. This includes his self-disclosure as "father," and therefore as personal. The Freudian model, therefore, in which the God-image is seen as a projection of the father-image, cannot be discounted in extrapolating the human and experiential meaning of this personal God and the "I-Thou" nature of one's relationship with him. At the same time the Jungian model helps us to avoid the hazard of absolutizing a particular set of historically conditioned symbols of the sacred or numinous by demonstrating that this particular set of symbols responds to needs and aspirations which are part of the universal structures of human existence. In this way the knowledge of God, though based on a particular historical revelatory event, is nevertheless perceived as being consistent with what is timeless and universal in human nature. At the same time the human meaningfulness of the Christian God-image is preserved without simply equating it with the reality which it symbolizes.

NOTES

1. Edward Glover, *Freud or Jung* (Cleveland: World Publishing Co., 1956), p. 163.

2.   Sigmund Freud, *The Future of an Illusion*, trans. James Strachey (New York: Norton, 1961), p. 31.

3.   Ibid., pp. 32–33.

4.   Ibid., pp. 40–41.

5.   Sigmund Freud, *The Ego and the Id*, trans. Joan Riviere (London: Hogarth Press, 1949), p. 45.

6.   Y. Masih, *Freudianism and Religion* (Calcutta: Thacker and Sphenk, 1964), pp. 214–15.

7.   See chapter 7 of R. S. Lee, *Freud and Christianity* (Hammondsworth, Eng.: Penguin, 1967).

8.   Sigmund Freud, *Civilization and Its Discontents*, trans. James Strachey (New York: Norton, 1961), p. 79.

9.   Peter Homans, "Toward a Psychology of Religion: By Way of Freud and Tillich," *Zygon* 2.1 (March 1967): 97–119.

10. See chapter 6 of Paul Tillich, *The Courage to Be* (London: Fontana, 1962).

11. See part 4 of Sigmund Freud, *Totem and Taboo: Resemblances between the Psychic Lives of Savages and Neurotics*, trans. A. A. Brill (New York: Random House, 1946).

12. Ana-Maria Rizzuto, *The Birth of the Living God* (Chicago: University of Chicago Press, 1979), p. 44.

13. Ibid.

14. See chapter 8 of Lee, *Freud and Christianity*.

15. Erik Erikson, *Childhood and Society* (New York: Norton, 1963), p. 250.

16. Erik Erikson, *Identity and the Life Cycle* (New York: Norton, 1980), pp. 62–63.

17. We are primarily concerned here with Erikson's emphasis on the significance of the role of the mother figure and the mode of adaptation of the first stage for religious development. It should be noted, however, that Erikson finds religious significance in later stages of growth in that religion may provide the ideology which is an essential ingredient in the adolescent's identity formation as well as in the "ego-integrity" that is the developmental task of old age. Cf. Erikson's *Young Man Luther*, and Peter Homans' "Erikson's Understanding of Religion," in *Childhood and Selfhood: Essays on Tradition, Religion and Modernity*, ed. Peter Homans (Lewisburg, Pa.: Bucknell University Press, 1978), pp. 241–48.

18. Erich Fromm, *The Sane Society* (Greenwich, Conn.: Fawcett Publications, 1965), pp. 42–46.

19. Ibid., pp. 48–50.

20. Ibid., p. 49.

21. Ibid., p. 50.

22. Ibid., p. 51.

23. Heije Faber, *Psychology of Religion*, trans. Margaret Kohl (Philadelphia: Westminster, 1975), p. 149.

24. Ibid., pp. 200–10.
25. Ibid., p. 262.
26. Ibid., p. 247.
27. *The Collected Works of C. G. Jung*, ed. Gerhard Adler, Michael Fordham, and Herbert Read, 20 vols. (London: Routledge and Kegan Paul, 1953–1979), 11:509. In this chapter all further quotations of Jung's writings are from the *Collected Works* (hereafter referred to as *CW*) and are cited in the text by volume and paragraph numbers.
28. Edward Edinger, *The Christian Archetype: A Jungian Commentary on the Life of Christ* (Toronto: Inner City Books, 1987), p. 112.
29. Charles Hanna, *The Face of the Deep: The Religious Ideas of C. G. Jung* (Philadelphia: Westminster, 1967), p. 85.
30. David Cox, *Jung and St. Paul* (London: Longmans Green and Co., 1959).
31. John E. Smith, *Experience and God* (New York: Oxford University Press, 1968).
32. Emmanuel Levinas, *Totality and Infinity*, trans. Alphonso Lingis (Pittsburgh: Duquesne University Press, 1969).
33. See chapter 3 of Smith, *Experience and God*.
34. See chapter 4 of Gordon Kaufman, *God the Problem* (Cambridge: Harvard University Press, 1972).
35. Ibid., p. 77.
36. Ibid., p. 78.
37. Paul Tillich, *The Protestant Era* (Chicago: University of Chicago Press, 1948), p. 89.
38. Smith, *Experience and God*, p. 86.
39. Kaufman, *God the Problem*, pp. 80–81.
40. Ibid., p. 78.
41. Martin Buber, *Eclipse of God* (New York: Harper and Row, 1957), p. 21.
42. Ibid., p. 45.
43. Smith, *Experience and God*, p. 85.
44. Ibid., pp. 84–85.
45. Levinas, *Totality and Infinity*, p. 40.
46. Ibid., pp. 43–45.
47. Ibid., p. 62.
48. Ibid., p. 77.
49. Ibid., pp. 79–80.
50. Ibid., p. 102.
51. Ibid., pp. 22–23.
52. Ibid., pp. 104–105.
53. Ibid., p. 41.
54. Ibid., p. 293.
55. Ibid., p. 279.
56. R. S. Lee, *Your Growing Child and Religion* (New York: Macmillan, 1963), pp. 66–67.

Chapter 7
The Problem of Morality

IN the most general terms, the question of natural theology is the question of a possible correlation or correspondence or proportionality between the human and the divine. Traditionally, this referred to the proportionality between the human capacity to know and God as an object of that knowledge; that is, to the human capacity to know something of the existence and nature of God apart from revelation. In the new style of natural theology which we have been discussing, the question of proportionality becomes the question of a possible correlation between the conditions of human nature and existence and what is known about God and the divine-human relationship through revelation and theological speculation on that revelation. In the course of our discussion we have observed at least two consequences of this new understanding of natural theology. In the first place, since the understanding of human nature and existence is not derived solely from philosophy but also from psychology and the social sciences, there exists the possibility of a psychologically based natural theology. In this study we have been concerned with the problem of constructing such a natural theology on the basis of the understanding of human existence which emerges from the psychological theories of Freud and Jung. Secondly, such an understanding of natural theology does not necessarily imply a teleological model of transcendence to the exclusion of the interpersonal model; that is, it does not imply totality to the exclusion of infinity.

In this chapter I want to illustrate a third consequence of this new understanding of natural theology, namely, the breadth of scope it gives to the question of proportionality. If natural theology deals with a possible correlation between the human condition and the broad scope of theological concepts derived from revelation, then this would include the theological understanding of the ethical relationship in which the believer stands to God and his neighbour. The application of the question of natural theology to the problem of Christian ethics might be expressed as follows: Is there a correlation between our understanding of human moral striving and the theological understanding of God or transcendence? This is the fundamental question in the debate on whether a rationally constructed ethical system is possible or whether ethics must have a religious foundation. In his book *Morality and Beyond* Paul Tillich has dealt with this question of the relationship of morality and religion in such a way as to exemplify, I believe, the type of natural theology we are discussing.

Tillich believes that the "conflict between reason-determined ethics and faith-determined ethics" is obsolete because "morality is intrinsically religious, as religion is intrinsically ethical," and therefore "neither is dependent on the other, and neither can be substituted for the other."[1] In answering the question in this way, he points to a correlation between the human striving to respond to the moral imperative and the notion of transcendence by arguing that even in the case of reason-determined ethics there is always present a religious or transcendent dimension. This religious dimension is to be found first of all in the unconditional character of the fundamental moral imperative. But what is the fundamental moral imperative? Tillich answers: "The moral imperative is the command to become what one potentially is, a *person* within a community of persons."[2] This answer is based on Tillich's analysis of the human condition as characterized by the split between one's essential self and existential self, between one's ideal and actual self. Hence this imperative may also be expressed as "the demand to become actually what one is essentially and therefore potentially."[3] What makes this moral imperative religious is the fact that, while it does not depend on divine revelation, neither is it the creation of human reason; it is the law of our own nature or being and thus has an unconditional character. Awareness of this imperative of self-actualization, whose source is our "true being" or "essential nature," is rooted in "the awareness of our belonging to a dimension that transcends our own finite freedom and our ability to affirm or to negate ourselves."[4] It issues from a source which transcends the finite, actual self and is therefore experienced as unconditional.

Tillich argues further that, if the fundamental moral imperative is the overcoming of estrangement from one's essential self and others, then it directs us towards participation in the other. Hence the source of moral commands is the command to love. It is, however, the agapeic quality of love which expresses "the self-transcendence of the religious element in love," for "agape transcends the finite possibilities of man."[5] The motive power, therefore, for moral action must also come from a source which transcends our limited, finite capacities. Commitment to the moral law merely confronts us with the split in our existence between the ideal and the actual. The ability to fulfill the law can only come from grace, that is, "the acceptance of the message that we are accepted."[6] Forgiveness of this existential condition and fulfillment of the moral ideal can only come from something above the law, from a healing power which overcomes the split between the essential and the actual. Again, therefore, morality is intrinsically religious because moral motivation is derived from a transcendent source.

But the new style of natural theology would enquire not only into the essentially religious character of morality—its correlation with transcendence—but also into the essential *humanness* of morality. In the context of a psychologically based natural theology, the question would be: Is there a correlation between the structure and dynamics of human personality and Christian morality, between the goal of authentic human growth and the Christian moral ideal? But what is the Christian moral ideal? Here we touch on the fundamental questions of Christian ethics: What is the content of Christian commitment? What is the criterion of the love, service, and obedience implied in faith? What is the norm by which the Christian is to make moral decisions? The answers to such questions are to be found in the moral consequences of that experience of grace and faith the dynamics of which we discussed in chapter 3, for if there is such a thing as a uniquely Christian morality its authentic expression must be the outcome of that religious experience which is fundamental to the Christian life. In the reflections which follow, I wish to explore the possible correlation between the goals of authentic human growth as proposed by Freud and Jung and the Christian moral ideal. In doing so, our discussion will follow a somewhat different pattern from that of the previous chapters. After examining the Christian moral ideal of altruistic, self-transcending love (agape) as a consequence of the experience of grace and faith, we shall then compare the meaning of that moral ideal with the meaning of the goals of human growth as described by Freud (Eros) and Jung (wholeness). Since, however, the relationship between the

Freudian Eros and the Christian agape has already been discussed
at some length in chapter 3, we shall content ourselves in this chapter
with a brief summary of that material.

Faith and Morality

In our discussion of the faith experience we saw that the moral law
is a cause of anxiety as long as the attempt to observe it arises from
motives of self-justification; that is, as long as an individual feels
that he must justify or render himself acceptable before God through
observance of the law. Faith is the antidote to this anxiety because
it involves the acceptance of justification as a free gift of God (grace).
This means that what results from the experience of grace and faith
is a new kind of relationship with God—a relationship which transcends the merely ethical and legalistic relationship of one who
stands "under the law." This new relationship is a *personal* relationship and, like any personal relationship, is based on an unconditional love and acceptance which need not and indeed cannot
be earned. At the basis of this relationship is the psychological truth
that self-realization is not the result of one's own isolated effort but
comes as a gift from without; it is the result of being accepted by
another. For the Christian this means that the transformation he
tries unsuccessfully to bring about in himself through moralistic
striving or legal observance is ultimately achieved only through
God's act of forgiveness and acceptance in Christ. In this way he
is liberated from the necessity of self-justification and is free to serve
God out of the spontaneous love and gratitude which result from
a personal relationship.

St. Paul sees the act of faith as making possible the transition from despair and anxiety to trust and confidence; from a legalistic to a personal relationship; from the bondage of sin to the freedom of grace; and, psychologically, from self-justifying motives to
self-transcending motives. In chapter 8 of Romans, Paul discusses
the vital principle of this transformation, of this new life and new
type of relationship. That vital and dynamic principle is the "gift
of the Spirit," and this indwelling of the Spirit is the basis of the
Christian's personal relationship with God. It is because "the Spirit
of God has made his home in you," he tells the Christians of Rome,
that they are constituted as "children of God" and able to address
God as "Abba, Father" (Rom. 8:8–17).

Christianity's claim to uniqueness is based, as we know, on its belief in the reality of a "new covenant" or relationship with God which has come about through the redemptive work of Christ and is appropriated by the believer through faith. This new relationship is neither the formal contract which God established with Abraham (Genesis 15) nor the legal covenant of Mount Sinai (Exodus 19) but a personal relationship with God in Christ. This is indicated in the prologue of the fourth gospel, which speaks of the different ways in which God has revealed himself: in nature (1:3); in the written law given through Moses (1:17); and finally in the most adequate human way—as a person: the Word, the principle of God's self-revelation, became flesh (1:14). God's ultimate self-revelation is in the form of a person—Jesus Christ—for in Christ the believer is called to a personal relationship with God. Thomas Aquinas describes the principle of this relationship—the Spirit or the third person of the Trinity—in two ways: as the bond between the Father and the Son, and as the substantial love of God.[7] The gift of the Spirit, which is the basis of the transforming power of faith, may therefore be thought of as having a twofold effect on the believer.

(1) Since the Holy Spirit is the bond between the Father and the Son, the gift of the Spirit implies a sharing in this bond or relationship. To be "in Christ" is to share in Christ's relationship with the Father. The believer, therefore, is given as a free gift the kind of justifying relationship with his God which previously he had tried to fashion and earn through his human attempts to observe the law. This involves a certain freedom from the law since he no longer depends on his success in keeping the law for winning God's acceptance. That acceptance has been given freely, and since the believer no longer has to use the law to "prove himself," the law loses its threatening and oppressive character. The one who lives "under grace" is liberated to keep the law for more altruistic, self-transcending motives; to keep the law not in order to earn a reward but out of gratitude for a gift already bestowed.

(2) Since the Holy Spirit is the substantial love of the Father and Son, the gift of the Spirit implies the gift of an inner capacity for love. "The love of God," writes St. Paul, "has been poured into our hearts by the Holy Spirit which has been given us" (Rom. 5:5). The Christian, therefore, believes that through the gift of God's Spirit he has received not only the Christian law of love but

a dynamic principle of life which gives him the inner capacity to do what the law of love commands. This implies a liberation from what Paul calls "the flesh," namely, the spirit of self-centredness and self-seeking into which one inevitably falls apart from the saving encounter with Christ and the gift of his Spirit. Joseph Fitzmeyer writes: "The Law proposed an ideal but did not enable man to arrive at it. Now all that is changed. Man has the Spirit that enables him to surmount the flesh and arrive at the goal that the Law once proposed."[8] The basic Christian imperative, therefore, is the Pauline injunction to follow the Spirit rather than the flesh (Gal. 5:16-18).

To summarize: The gift of the Spirit involves sharing a personal relationship with God in Christ and receiving an inner power or capacity to love. Consequently it involves a twofold liberation: liberation from the bondage of law since the believer's relationship with God is personal rather than legal; liberation from the bondage of "the flesh" since the believer is given the inner capacity to love. St. Paul reminds us, however, that the bondage of sin or the flesh is not experienced as such apart from the law (Rom. 7:7-13). Thus he locates the liberating, transcending, and transforming power of faith in the experience of freedom from the law (Rom. 7:4-6). But in what sense is the Christian liberated from the moral law? Certainly not in the sense that the moral law has been abrogated, for the commandments still express valid moral principles. In Paul's words, "the Law is sacred and what it commands is sacred, just and good" (Rom. 7:12). What the Christian is liberated from, however, is the "oppression" of the law, that is, the necessity of justifying himself by observing and fulfilling the law. Thus the believer is liberated from the law, not objectively, for the law is still objectively valid, but rather subjectively in that he acquires a new attitude to the law. This new attitude is based on three basic premises which therefore appear as the foundation for the self-transcending quality of faith.

(1) The law is transcended by the believer's personal relationship with God. Law is, by its very nature, limiting. It defines exactly what one must do or not do. It creates, therefore, a legalistic relationship with the lawgiver. But a personal relationship cannot be expressed in law, cannot be codified. Because it is personal, it is unlimited and "open-ended," that is, subject to growth and change. There are no artificial limits to the love and service rendered to

a loved one as there is to the obedience due to an authority. Though there may be, for instance, mutually agreed upon rules governing the shared responsibilities of a husband and wife, it would be ridiculous to think of such rules as exhausting the meaning of their relationship. At the personal level what is required of them is an ongoing sensitivity to each other's changing needs—a sensitivity which cannot be codified. In the same way, the Christian, while recognizing the objective validity of the law, does not make the mistake of thinking that a written law could ever adequately express his relationship with God in Christ, which is personal. For this reason there is no room for complacency, since the mere keeping of the law does not exhaust the possibilities for love and service in this or any other personal relationship. Having kept the law, he still considers himself an "unprofitable servant" (Luke 17:10), and with the rich young man must still ask, "What more do I need to do?"

(2) Because he is justified by the free gift of God and his faith in that gift, the Christian no longer depends on keeping the law to justify himself before God. The New Testament message is that salvation is never the result of keeping the law. It must be a gift. St. Paul points out that Abraham was justified (Gen. 15:6) solely by his faith in God's promise, for he lived before the giving of the law on Mount Sinai, and the giving of the law does not annul the justifying power of God's promise or Abraham's faith. The Christian believer, like Abraham, is justified by his faith in God's promise and not by his own moral rectitude (Gal. 3:21–22).

(3) Finally, since justification is a free gift of God, the moral effort of the Christian is not the cause of his friendship with God but its effect. The personal relationship which he enjoys through faith is not the result of morality; rather, his moral effort is the result of his personal relationship with God. In traditional language, good works are the effect, not the cause, of justification. The moral life of the believer is his response to the gift of justification and salvation. Likewise, his moral failures are looked upon not so much as the breaking of a law imposed from without, but as a failure to live up to the demands of a personal relationship to which he has freely committed himself—as a failure to love. It is only within the context of such a commitment and relationship that one may legitimately reduce all of Christian morality to Augustine's injunction: "Love and do what you will."[9]

If, therefore, Christian morality is a consequence of the experience of grace and faith, it is a morality based on the premise of "freedom from the law." Unless one wishes to interpret this freedom in absolute terms and subscribe to a form of antinomianism, it means that the moral law, though valid as an expression of universal moral principles, may be relativized in concrete situations by the presence of a more ultimate moral criterion—the responsibility of faith. Authentic Christian morality transcends all codes of ethics, all universal moral principles, and all forms of legalism. In one word, it is personalist rather than legalistic since the ultimate moral criterion is not a written law but fidelity to a Person and to a personal relationship. What is true of personal relationships in general is true also of the divine-human relationship—the responsibilities of the relationship ultimately cannot be codified. The history of Christian morality, however, reveals a tendency to regress to a legalistic form of morality. Legalism is a distortion of Christian morality precisely because it relates the individual, not to a Person or to persons, but to abstract and impersonal laws and principles. As Marc Oraison has pointed out, this abstraction is maintained for the psychological reason that it protects the individual from the risk of real human encounter.[10] Anything other than a morality of law is seen by the legalist as a threat to his security. In keeping the letter of the law, the legalist aims at the kind of security and certainty that one can never have in a personal relationship—the certainty of being always in the right. In doing so he regresses to a state of preoccupation with himself and his own moral perfection which is the antithesis of that spontaneous, self-transcending love which is the Christian moral ideal.

The search for a "new morality" is, in actuality, a reaction against this legalizing tendency among Christians; it is a search, not for a new morality in any absolute sense, but for a return to and restatement of an authentic Christian morality. It is the search for the authentic alternative to legalism, for an answer to the question: What does it mean to follow the "spirit" rather than the "letter"? This question is not adequately answered by reverting, as Joseph Fletcher does, to a pragmatic type of situationism.[11] If the "spirit" in question refers to that gift of God's Spirit which liberates and transforms the believer and without which the moral ideal of self-transcending agape is impossible of achievement, then we must say that the Christian moral ideal is humanly impossible.

This is what Fletcher ignores in reducing all of Christian morality to one universal absolute—the law of love, to do the most loving thing in any given situation. He agrees that the Christian moral ideal is agape but distorts its meaning by defining it as the only kind of love which can be commanded, since it represents, for Fletcher, a kind of benevolent love, a love commanded by the will which does not necessarily involve "liking" those whom we love. He thereby rejects the understanding of agape as precisely the kind of love that cannot be commanded since to love another for his own sake and free of self-concern requires a kind of self-transcendence or freedom from self-preoccupation which only the experience of grace and faith can effect.

   In the end, therefore, situationism becomes the very thing it wants to avoid—a form of legalism. As long as the moral ideal of love is understood as something which can be commanded, then rather than replacing law with love, it has replaced many laws with one law. Insofar as it settles for a love that can be commanded, it represents a morality of law, for it ignores the fact that Christian morality transcends law as such, including the law of love. The experience of grace and faith creates the possibility of a love which does not have to be commanded. At the same time, the altruistic ideal of agape is never fully realized, so that there remains a tragic dimension to the moral life—the tragedy of knowing that we do not do the good we ought to do and that sometimes we must settle for doing the lesser of two evils. It is this tragedy which situationism tends to eliminate by reducing the moral ideal to something which can be commanded. If one can be satisfied that one has done the good by doing the most loving thing, then the possibility of a bad conscience has been eliminated and the certainty and security of the legalist recovered.

Freud and Christian Morality

To return to what I have suggested might be the question of natural theology in regard to Christian ethics: Is there a correlation between the goal of authentic human growth and the Christian moral ideal? It is obvious from our brief discussion of the Christian moral ideal—agape—that it points beyond a morality of law. We have seen in chapters 2 and 3 that, in the Freudian view, the goal of authentic human growth is also unattainable through observance

of law, that is, through the process of civilization. We may summarize our earlier discussion of the similarities between the Freudian
Eros and the Christian agape by recalling that Freudian theory and
Christianity are in basic agreement on the following points: (1) The
goal of both human and religious growth is the fullness of life. (2)
In both cases, life is conceived of as an interpersonal reality. The
Freudian Eros represents a unifying force which brings together
individual units of life to form a greater unity. The Christian agape
represents a spontaneous, self-transcending kind of love, free of
self-preoccupation, which makes possible the realization of that unity
which is the goal of Eros. (3) In both the Freudian and Christian
view, this goal of life is beyond human achievement. Both the pursuit of moral ideals through observance of law and the repression
of the death instinct through the process of civilization lead paradoxically to a condition which both Freud and St. Paul describe
as "death." Both law and civilization lead to the experience of death
in the form of guilt—a death which St. Paul sees as the necessary
preamble to the life-producing experience of grace and faith.

We may conclude, therefore, that although Freud did not
share St. Paul's conviction about the possibility of life through grace
and faith and the gift of the Spirit, there is fundamental agreement
on these two points: the Christian moral ideal—agape—and the
goal of authentic human growth—Eros—are experientially the same
(oneness or unity); and both the Christian agape and the Freudian
Eros represent *transcendent* goals of human becoming in that they
are goals beyond human achievement. This latter point should be
instructive for those involved in Christian moral education. Educators in this field have been greatly influenced in recent years by
the research that has been done in the field of cognitive moral development, especially that of Lawrence Kohlberg.[12] Kohlberg traces
the development of moral decision-making through six stages which
fall within three general levels—the pre-conventional, conventional,
and post-conventional. At the post-conventional level the individual
moves from stage 5—a "social contract" type of morality stressing
the rights of individuals within a given society—to stage 6, in which
moral decisions are made on the basis of universal ethical principles
which apply to all of humanity.

As valuable as Kohlberg's work is in helping the educator
assess the appropriateness of instructional material in the light of
the student's level of cognitive moral maturity, one has the impres-

sion that some religious educators view the six stages as a pattern of *Christian* moral development. Such a view ignores the fact that the development of the Christian moral agent involves more than the development of the capacity for moral reasoning. The fulfillment of the Christian moral ideal is, as we have seen, impossible apart from the transforming experience of grace and faith and the gift of God's Spirit. Even though an individual may have arrived at the cognitive moral maturity of stage 6, his situation remains analogous to that of the person who is still "under the law"; the universal moral principles of this stage represent, in the Christian view, an ideal impossible of fulfillment apart from the liberating and self-transcending experience of grace and faith. It is significant also that the "golden rule" is the most frequently used example of this stage 6 moral reasoning, for it falls short of the Christian moral ideal. Though Christ refers to the injunction to "love your neighbour as yourself" (Matt. 22:39), he does so by way of expressing the moral ideal of the Mosaic law. But the "new commandment" which expresses Jesus' own moral teaching is to love one another "just as I have loved you" (John 13:34). Christian morality cannot be understood simply as a law of love; it is a love which is beyond human achievement and therefore cannot be understood apart from the religious experience which makes that ideal to some extent possible of fulfillment. To speak enthusiastically of "6th-stage Christians" as if this were somehow the epitome of Christian maturity is to trivialize the Christian moral ideal.

Jung and Christian Morality

If Eros represents a goal of human growth which is consistent with the Christian moral ideal of agape, the same may be said of the concept of wholeness or selfhood which Jung sees as the goal of the individuation process. For St. Paul, to live "under the law," that is, to pursue self-justification through moral observance, leads to the experience of "death" as opposed to life. Likewise for Freud, the law in the form of civilization, which is a "process in the service of Eros," leads paradoxically to the experience of death in the form of guilt as opposed to life. Faith, to the extent that it makes agape and therefore life in the Christian sense possible, is to be understood as the solution to the conflict of law versus sin (St. Paul) or the conflict of Eros versus death (Freud). This is the conflict experienced by one who is "under the law," and it is this conflict which Jung described as the conflict of wholeness versus perfection. For Jung, conscious pursuit of moral perfection through observance of collective moral norms brings one into conflict with the unconscious goal of the total personality, that union of opposites, of conscious and unconscious contents, implied in the word "wholeness." Jung's insistence that one must become reconciled with the unconscious side of personality—including the shadow or dark side—implies a moral ideal which transcends a legalistic morality of law, which is based on the repression of the shadow in favour of a persona which conforms to the conscious moral ideal, but which does not represent one's total personality.

The conflict experienced by one who is "under the law" exists at two levels. At one level it is experienced as a conflict between knowledge and will—between one's knowledge of the good as expressed in the moral law and one's inability to fulfill the ideal proposed by the law. At a deeper level it is experienced as an awareness of the inadequacy of the law and the ethical life as such. In other words, even if one were to fulfill the moral law perfectly, it would not be enough. Why is this so? As a religious answer to this question we could say with Sören Kierkegaard that the ethical life, even if lived to the limits of its possibilities, falls short of the religious (personal) relationship with the Absolute which the religious person strives for.

Universal ethical norms reduce everyone to the same level and subject everyone to the same demands. This is opposed to the unique set of responsibilities which the individual would experience in the context of a personal relationship with his God, and which relativize universal ethical principles. The ethical life, Kierkegaard argues, cannot satisfy our deepest religious aspirations; it can only serve as a necessary prelude to authentic religious existence.

In the same way, Jung, in what we might construe as a psychological answer to our question, points out that the pursuit of moral perfection does not satisfy our deepest human aspirations. Moral perfection represents the goal of only the conscious dimension of personality; the personality as a whole seeks wholeness or completeness rather than perfection. Wholeness, as we have seen, involves the assimilation of unconscious contents—including the shadow or dark side of personality—into our conscious behaviour and attitudes. In Jung's view, therefore, authentic morality has as its goal the achieving of wholeness—a goal which, in some real sense, goes "beyond good and evil."

Jung proposed that "ethics," namely, obedience to collective moral norms, was based on the repression of the shadow, since the shadow represents all that is incompatible with the morally perfect persona one wants to project. This repression has two negative consequences. In the first place, it creates tension as well as physical and psychic symptoms because part of one's total self is denied expression. This tension arises not only because the individual must become conscious of his dark side and dispel illusions about himself, but frequently because the repressed content turns out to be "the stone which the builders rejected"—something necessary for healthy living. Secondly, the repression of the shadow is harmful to interpersonal life since the shadow which is not recognized as part of oneself is then projected onto others. As we saw in our discussion of the sacrament of penance, the projection of the shadow is disruptive of community since the other onto whom the shadow is projected becomes a source of evil, someone to be feared, or against whom one must protect oneself. Such defensive barriers tend to destroy interpersonal life because they isolate the individual from his environment. The ego-defensiveness arising from projection is another illustration of the self-preoccupation which acts as an obstacle to the spontaneous, self-transcending love which is the Christian moral ideal.

In the Jungian view, an authentic morality would aim at wholeness rather than perfection according to collective ethical norms. Such a morality would have the following characteristics which would seem to be consistent with the Christian moral ideal. In the first place, the starting point of such an ethic would be the recognition and assimilation into consciousness of the shadow. Jung lists the following consequences of such a recognition of the shadow: it creates a sense of wholeness or completeness since it involves union with a previously rejected dimension of oneself; it leads also to the withdrawal of those self-justifying projections which result from repression of the shadow; and because projections are withdrawn, the barriers to interpersonal life or community are removed. Analogous to this is the Christian concept of repentance as the starting point of the Christian life. Like the recognition of the shadow, repentance is the conscious admission of the evil in oneself, which also leads to the abandoning of a false legalistic sense of moral superiority and the creation of authentic community.

When one attempts to describe the features of authentic Christian morality within the context of Jungian theory, the question arises: What is the meaning of "assimilation" of the shadow in reference to the Christian act of repentance? Does it mean that an individual simply abandons his conscious moral principles and acts out his propensity for evil for the sake of wholeness? Erich Neumann's construction of a "new ethic" on the basis of Jungian theory seems to result in a kind of Jungian "situationism." All morality is reduced to one criterion: what promotes wholeness or integration is good; what leads to disintegration is evil. In the light of this criterion all other moral absolutes and all notions of intrinsic goodness or evil are relativized.[13] Jung himself, however, seems to be more at pains to caution us that the assimilation of unconscious contents is not a surrender to those contents, but a new level of consciousness in which the hard won gains of the growth of consciousness—including the development of moral principles—are not simply abandoned. I believe that the following points reflect Jung's understanding of the ethical consequences of the recognition of the shadow, which in turn correlate with the ethical consequences of the Christian faith experience.

(1) As we have seen, the recognition of the shadow, which for the Christian is the act of repentance, leads to a renewed sense of wholeness or completeness. This holds true only if the recognition of the dark side of one's personality involves a real acceptance of it as part of one's total identity. The believer's "consciousness of sin" is not a movement towards wholeness unless that sin is accepted as part of his total self and not seen as something to be eliminated through moral effort. In other words, self-knowledge must be completed by self-acceptance. In the Christian faith experience that self-acceptance is made possible by grace—God's unconditional acceptance. It is this acceptance of one's total self—including the shadow or dark side—which Jung calls "the essence of the moral problem and the acid test of one's whole outlook on life."[14] He goes on to argue that the prerequisite for loving one's enemies is to first love the enemy within oneself, that is, the rejected, dark aspect of oneself. Morality begins with the recognition that "I myself stand in need of the alms of my own kindness—that I myself am the enemy who must be loved," for only he who has fully accepted himself has 'unprejudiced objectivity.' "[15] It is the experience of divine acceptance resulting in self-acceptance which makes possible the

"unprejudiced objectivity" of the believer's love for others; makes possible, that is, the freedom from self-concern which creates the possibility of altruistic love.

(2) Recognition of the shadow brings to the light of consciousness those undesirable aspects of one's personality of which one was previously unaware. The conscious recognition of such dark aspects brings them under greater conscious control. As Jung has pointed out, that which is unconsciously repressed tends to act in an autonomous way to disrupt personal and social life. In Jung's view, evil cannot be done away with just as in the Christian view sin, understood as that basic egoism which is the source of moral transgressions, cannot be eliminated. It can only be consciously recognized and submitted to grace and forgiveness. In this way one gains some measure of conscious control over it. As June Singer remarks, "In the psyche, we cannot 'dispose' of dangerous or destructive aspects of ourselves, we can only know of their presence and how they tend to function. If we work at it we may be able to transform these dark elements from something virulent to something manageable."[16]

(3) Recognition and assimilation of the shadow points to a new type of ethic in which moral decisions are made according to a criterion other than the conscious differentiation between good and evil as represented in ethical codes. We have seen that authentic Christian morality does not dispense with the law but recognizes a higher authority, namely, the responsibilities experienced in the personal relationship of faith. In the same way, from the Jungian perspective, a morality to which the total personality can respond is a morality whose aim is wholeness rather than perfection and which offers, therefore, a moral criterion which transcends and relativizes the conscious collective ethical norms. For Jung, authentic morality involves obedience to the "inner voice" of the unconscious, which directs the growth of personality towards the goal of wholeness. Such a moral ideal resembles the Christian moral ideal in two respects. In the first place, it is an "internal" morality; that is, it points to an internal criterion for moral decision-making as opposed to an external moral code or authority. Moral decisions are not simply acts of obedience to an external authority but come from within. Christianity speaks of following the Spirit rather than the letter; Jung, of obedience to the inner voice of the unconscious, that is, of the self, which may oppose the ego's rational concep-

tions of good and evil. In each case the external law is relativized
by this more ultimate criterion.

Secondly, the moral consequences of both the recognition
of the shadow and of the Christian faith experience suggest a morality which is "beyond good and evil," that is, which transcends the
narrow conceptions of good and evil to be found in code morality
and in our conscious differentiations between good and evil. For
Jung, the unconscious unites and synthesizes what consciousness
differentiates just as, for the Christian, the legal and moral dis-
tinctions between good and evil do not necessarily correspond to
the will of God or what Kierkegaard called the "absolute duty
toward God." This absolute duty relativizes one's commonly held
ethical principles, so that in concrete situations the ethical norm
may be suspended (though not abolished) out of obedience to the
will of God. "The ethical relation," writes Kierkegaard, "is reduced
to a relative position in contrast with the absolute relation to
God."[17] But, for Kierkegaard, such moral decisions in which the
demands of faith lead one to act contrary to the moral law are made
in "fear and trembling," and Jung agrees. In a letter to David
Cox he states: "To be alone with God is highly suspect . . . because
the will of God can be terrible and can isolate you against your
family and friends. . . . And yet how can there be religion without
the experience of the Divine Will? Things are comparatively easy
as long as He wants nothing but the fulfillment of His laws, but
what if He wants you to break them as He may do equally
well?"[18]

The Freudian concept of Eros and the Jungian concept of
wholeness represent goals of authentic human growth. But, like
the Christian ideal of agape, they are *transcendent* goals in that they
transcend the possibilities of a life which seeks its perfection and
fulfillment in observance of ethical laws.

NOTES

1. Paul Tillich, *Morality and Beyond* (New York: Harper and Row,
     1966), p. 15.
2. Ibid., p. 19.
3. Ibid., p. 20.
4. Ibid., p. 25.

5. Ibid., p. 40.
6. Ibid., p. 54.
7. *Summa Theologiae*, Pt. 1, Qu. 37–38.
8. *Jerome Biblical Commentary* (Englewood Cliffs, N.J.: Prentice Hall, 1968), 53:82.
9. *In Epistolam Joannis at Parthos Tractatus*, 8:8.
10. Marc Oraison, *Morality for Our Time*, trans. Nels Challe (Garden City, N.Y.: Doubleday, 1969), pp. 59–64.
11. Joseph Fletcher, *Situation Ethics: The New Morality* (Philadelphia: Westminster, 1966).
12. Lawrence Kohlberg, "Moral Development," in *International Encyclopedia of the Social Sciences*, 18 vols. (New York: Macmillan and Free Press, 1968), 10:483–94.
13. Erich Neumann, *Depth Psychology and a New Ethic*, trans. Eugene Rolfe (New York: Harper and Row, 1973), pp. 126–27.
14. *The Collected Works of C. G. Jung*, ed. Gerhard Adler, Michael Fordham, and Herbert Read, 20 vols. (London: Routledge and Kegan Paul, 1953–1979), 11:520.
15. Jung, *Collected Works*, 11:520–21.
16. June Singer, *Boundaries of the Soul: The Practice of Jung's Psychology* (Garden City, N.Y.: Anchor Books, 1973), p. 160.
17. Sören Kierkegaard, *"Fear and Trembling" and "The Sickness unto Death,"* trans. Walter Lowrie (Princeton: Princeton University Press, 1968), p. 81.
18. Quoted in H. R. Philp, *Jung and the Problem of Evil* (London: Rockliff, 1958), p. 232.

Bibliography

PSYCHOLOGY OF RELIGION AS NATURAL THEOLOGY

Braaten, Carl. *The Future of God*. New York: Harper and Row, 1969.

Carter, John D., and Bruce Narramore. *The Integration of Psychology and Theology*. Grand Rapids, Mich.: Zondervan, 1979.

Cobb, John B., Jr. *A Christian Natural Theology*. London: Lutterworth Press, 1965.

Farnsworth, Kirk E. *Integrating Psychology and Theology*. Washington: University Press of America, 1981.

Fromm, Erich. *You Shall Be As Gods*. New York: Holt, Rinehart and Winston, 1966.

Gilkey, Langdon. *Naming the Whirlwind*. New York: Bobbs-Merrill, 1969.

Hartshorne, Charles. *A Natural Theology for Our Time*. Lasalle, Ill.: Open Court, 1967.

Hiltner, Seward. "The Psychological Understanding of Religion." *Crozer Quarterly* 24 (1947): 3-36.

Kaufman, Gordon. *God the Problem*. Cambridge: Harvard University Press, 1972.

Louth, Andrew. "Barth and the Problem of Natural Theology." *Downside Review* 87 (1969): 268-77.

McDargh, John. "Theological Uses of Psychology: Retrospective and Prospective." *Horizons* 12 (1985): 247-64.

Macquarrie, John. *Principles of Christian Theology*. New York: Scribner's, 1966.

Murray, John Courtney. *The Problem of God*. New Haven: Yale University Press, 1964.

Progoff, Ira. *The Death and Rebirth of Psychology*. New York: McGraw-Hill, 1956.

Schleiermacher, Friedrich. *On Religion: Speeches to Its Cultured Despisers*. Trans. John Oman. New York: Harper Torchbooks, 1958.

Tillich, Paul. *The Courage to Be*. London: Fontana, 1962.

_____. *Theology of Culture*. New York: Oxford, 1964.

Torrance, T. F. "The Problem of Natural Theology in the Thought of Karl Barth." *Religious Studies* 6 (1970): 121–35.

FREUD AND CHRISTIANITY

Bettelheim, Bruno. *Freud and Man's Soul*. New York: Knopf, 1983.

Brown, Norman O. *Life against Death: The Psychoanalytic Meaning of History*. New York: Random House, 1959.

Dubarle, André-Marie. *The Biblical Doctrine of Original Sin*. Trans. E. M. Stewart. New York: Herder and Herder, 1967.

Duquoc, Christian. "New Approaches to Original Sin." Trans. Joe Cuneen. *Cross Currents* Summer 1978: 189–200.

Erikson, Erik. *Identity and the Life Cycle*. New York: Norton, 1980.

Freud, Sigmund. *Beyond the Pleasure Principle*. Trans. James Strachey. New York: Bantam Books, 1967.

——————. *Civilization and Its Discontents*. Trans. James Strachey. New York: Norton, 1961.

——————. "The Ego and the Id." In *The Standard Edition of the Complete Psychological Works of Sigmund Freud*. Gen. ed. James Strachey. 24 vols. London: Hogarth Press, 1953–1974. 19:1–66.

——————. *The Future of an Illusion*. Trans. James Strachey. New York: Norton, 1961.

——————. "The Instincts and Their Vicissitudes." In his *Collected Papers*. Ed. Joan Riviere. 5 vols. London: Hogarth Press, 1924–1950. 4:60–83.

——————. "New Introductory Lectures on Psychoanalysis." In *The Standard Edition of the Complete Psychological Works of Sigmund Freud*. 22:1–182.

——————. *An Outline of Psychoanalysis*. Trans. James Strachey. New York: Norton, 1949.

——————. *Totem and Taboo: Resemblances between the Psychic Lives of Savages and Neurotics*. Trans. A. A. Brill. New York: Random House, 1946.

Fromm, Erich. *The Crisis of Psychoanalysis*. Greenwich, Conn.: Fawcett Publications, 1970.

——————. *The Heart of Man: Its Genius for Good and Evil*. New York: Harper and Row, 1964.

Homans, Peter. *Theology after Freud*. Indianapolis: Bobbs-Merrill, 1970.

Lee, R. S. *Freud and Christianity*. Harmondsworth, Eng.: Penguin, 1967.

Lyonnet, Stanislas. "St. Paul: Liberty and Law." In *The Bridge: A Yearbook of Judaeo-Christian Studies*. Ed. John M. Oesterreicher. New York: Pantheon Books, 1962. 4:229–51.

McDermott, Brian O., S.J. "The Theology of Original Sin: Recent Developments." *Theological Studies* 38.3 (1977): 478–512.

MacIsaac, Sharon. *Freud and Original Sin*. New York: Paulist Press, 1974.

Marcuse, Herbert. *Eros and Civilization: A Philosophical Inquiry into Freud*. Boston: Beacon, 1955.

Meissner, W. *Psychoanalysis and Religious Experience*. New Haven: Yale University Press, 1984.

Monden, Louis, S.J. *Sin, Liberty, and Law*. Trans. Joseph Donceel, S.J. New York: Sheed and Ward, 1965.

Ricoeur, Paul. *Freud and Philosophy: An Essay on Interpretation*. Trans. Denis Savage. New Haven: Yale University Press, 1970.

Vandervelde, G. *Original Sin: Two Major Trends in Catholic Reinterpretation*. Amsterdam: Rodopi, 1975.

JUNG AND CHRISTIANITY

Brown, Clifford. *Jung's Hermeneutic of Doctrine*. Chico, Calif.: Scholars Press, 1981.

Clift, Wallace B. *Jung and Christianity: The Challenge of Reconciliation*. New York: Crossroad, 1982.

Cox, David. *Jung and St. Paul*. London: Longmans Green and Co., 1959.

Dourley, John. *The Illness That We Are: A Jungian Critique of Christianity*. Toronto: Inner City Books, 1984.

——————. *C. G. Jung and Paul Tillich: The Psyche as Sacrament*. Toronto: Inner City Books, 1981.

Edinger, Edward. *The Bible and the Psyche: Individuation Symbolism in the Old Testament*. Toronto: Inner City Books, 1986.

——————. *The Christian Archetype: A Jungian Commentary on the Life of Christ*. Toronto: Inner City Books, 1987.

——————. *The Creation of Consciousness*. Toronto: Inner City Books, 1984.

Fordham, Frieda. *An Introduction to Jung's Psychology*. Harmondsworth, Eng.: Penguin, 1966.

Hanna, Charles. *The Face of the Deep: The Religious Ideas of C. G. Jung*. Philadelphia: Westminster, 1967.

Homans, Peter. *Jung in Context: Modernity and the Making of Psychology*. Chicago: University of Chicago Press, 1979.

Jacobi, Jolande. *The Psychology of C. G. Jung*. London: Routledge and Kegan Paul, 1968.

Jaffe, Aniela. *The Myth of Meaning*. Trans. R.F.C. Hull. New York: Penguin, 1975.

Jung, C. G. "Aion: Contributions to the Symbolism of the Self." In *The Collected Works of C. G. Jung.* Ed. Gerhard Adler, Michael Fordham, and Herbert Read. 20 vols. London: Routledge and Kegan Paul, 1953–1979. Vol. 9. Pt. 2.

——————. "Answer to Job." *Collected Works.* Vol. 11.

——————. "Archetypes of the Collective Unconscious." *Collected Works.* Vol. 9, Pt. 1.

——————. "Basic Postulates of Analytical Psychology." *Collected Works.* Vol. 8.

——————. "On the Nature of the Psyche." *Collected Works.* Vol. 8.

——————. "A Psychological Approach to the Dogma of the Trinity." *Collected Works.* Vol. 11.

——————. "Psychology and Religion." *Collected Works.* Vol. 11.

——————. "Psychotherapists or the Clergy." *Collected Works.* Vol. 11.

——————. "The Role of the Unconscious." *Collected Works.* Vol. 10.

——————. "The Spiritual Problem of Modern Man." *Collected Works.* Vol. 10.

——————. "The Structure of the Psyche." *Collected Works.* Vol. 8.

——————. "Symbols of Transformation." *Collected Works.* Vol. 5.

——————. "Transformation Symbolism in the Mass." *Collected Works.* Vol. 11.

——————. "Two Essays on Analytical Psychology." *Collected Works.* Vol. 7.

Moreno, Antonio. *Jung, Gods and Modern Man.* Notre Dame, Ind.: University of Notre Dame Press, 1970.

Philp, H. R. *Jung and the Problem of Evil.* London: Rockliff, 1958.

Stern, Paul. *C. G. Jung: The Haunted Prophet.* New York: George Braziller, 1976.

Tillich, Paul. *A History of Christian Thought.* London: SCM Press, 1968.

White, Victor. *God and the Unconscious.* London: Fontana, 1960.

FREUD OR JUNG?

Buber, Martin. *Eclipse of God.* New York: Harper and Row, 1957.

Erikson, Erik. *Childhood and Society.* New York: Norton, 1963.

Faber, Heije. *Psychology of Religion.* Trans. Margaret Kohl. Philadelphia: Westminster, 1975.

Fletcher, Joseph. *Situation Ethics: The New Morality.* Philadelphia: Westminster, 1966.

Glover, Edward. *Freud or Jung*. Cleveland: World Publishing Co., 1956.

Lee, R. S. *Your Growing Child and Religion*. New York: Macmillan, 1963.

Levinas, Emmanuel. *Totality and Infinity*. Trans. Alphonso Lingis. Pittsburgh: Duquesne University Press, 1969.

Neumann, Erich. *Depth Psychology and a New Ethic*. Trans. Eugene Rolfe. New York: Harper and Row, 1973.

Oraison, Marc. *Morality for Our Time*. Trans. Nels Challe. Garden City, N.Y.: Doubleday, 1969.

Rizzuto, Ana-Maria. *The Birth of the Living God*. Chicago: University of Chicago Press, 1979.

Smith, John E. *Experience and God*. New York: Oxford University Press, 1968.

Tillich, Paul. *Morality and Beyond*. New York: Harper and Row, 1966.